How to Live in Italy

Essays on the charms and complications
of living in paradise

Rebecca Helm-Ropelato

ISBN-13: 978-1478100539

Cover design by Lorenzo De Tomasi (Isotype.org)
Cover photographs by Rebecca Helm-Ropelato

For Franco

The gentle reader will never, never know what a consummate ass he can become until he goes abroad...

MARK TWAIN *THE INNOCENTS ABROAD*

Contents

PART THREE: OBSERVING ITALIANS

Introduction

Where do you live?

This question popped up in my mind repeatedly a few years ago during the minor displacement confusion of three weeks we spent in temporary quarters nearby while some major renovation work was underway on our apartment.

Contemplation of *Where do I live?* can pose itself as a kind of involuntary meditation for an ex-pat. Response to the question sets off a natural thought sequence: I live in another country. I have left my own country. Why?

Often the answer is straightforward. I'm here because of a turn of events such as a career opportunity or job transfer. Or as in my case, it can be a marriage. Many ex-pats have made the choice primarily based on a desire to live abroad, perhaps in a particular place they have long dreamed about.

But, at bottom, it's a voluntary choice, to some degree anyway.

Those few years ago during our temporary dislocation, I began a self-query of why I've made the choices I have about where I live. Leaving aside the larger question of Italy versus the US, I focused on other aspects. What gave rise to my preferences when we chose the location of our new home two years ago? What drew me to the particular town, the particular neighborhood, the particular street, the particular apartment?

The answer that eventually came surprised me. It arose as a useful update in my personal awareness: I live somewhere between my own aspirations and those of my parents. Some of their values, hopes and ambitions I carry with me always. And to these I've added some of my very own.

This understanding arrived via a recollection of a specific image, a vivid memory from childhood. It is a memory that encapsulates my personal life journey, as I think may be true for most of us if we decide to time travel backwards to our early ideas and dreams.

For much of my childhood, we lived in a house in the country. Quiet, green, rural, miles from the nearest town, far, far from any big cities, bright lights. Except for an occasional road trip, crowded into the family car with my brothers and sisters to visit friends in a neighboring state, it was the only world I knew. On warm summer days, sometimes I would flop down lazily on the grass, as children do, and stare up at the blue sky and high white clouds. And sometimes way up there, so far away it was only a barely discernible form, I would see a plane flying by, on its way from somewhere to somewhere.

As this image played through my mind during my ex-pat meditation, I understood all these many years later what was in my child's mind then – I wanted to follow that plane. And so I have.

All this to say that the articles and essays in this book are written especially for anyone who also once dreamed, or still dreams, of *following that plane*. For at the heart of that fantasy – if the dreamers are like me – is not only a driving curiosity about faraway places and the people who live there, but also a curiosity about themselves if they lived there.

Preface

The articles and essays in this collection were written during my first ten years in Italy, following my move here from California. Some were published in US newspapers. Others are revised versions of selected posts from my first website, that is exclusively devoted to Italy, Italians and their culture. And some essays are being published for the first time here.

Regarding the book's title, *How to Live in Italy*, it can be read in various ways. First, of course, many of these pieces recount my actual experiences of learning how to live here in Italy, in a country and language different from my own. The title, however, is intended also as a kind of word play, both poetic and tongue-in-cheek. Poetic in the sense that Italians especially have long been praised for knowing how to appreciate and enjoy daily living. And tongue-in-cheek in the sense of recognizing my awkward ways at times in the new culture I have entered.

As to the order of the content, the pieces are grouped generally by topic, rather than chronologically. This lends greater coherence, hopefully, to the whole.

PART ONE

Learning curves

An unalterable and unquestioned law of the musical world required that the German text of French operas sung by Swedish artists should be translated into Italian for the clearer understanding of English-speaking audiences.

EDITH WHARTON *THE AGE OF INNOCENCE*

1

The L.A. Effect

*Basking in the city's peculiar radiance
in the hills outside of Rome*

During the almost three decades I called Los Angeles home, I became accustomed, as Angelenos do when traveling, to the lame jokes about earthquakes and California crazies, the raised eyebrows from those who regard L.A. as an X-rated phantasm, and to the look of awe at times in the eyes of some dreamers, young and old, longing to explore the city's legendary myth. Revealing where I was from always evoked reaction. Since I have moved away, it has been the same.

I now live in Lariano, a tiny town in the countryside south of Rome. I moved here almost four years ago after marrying an Italian. When he suggested we live in Italy rather than the United States, I yielded without much struggle. I envisioned living in a traditional Italian villa, one of old, heavy stone construction – a stereotypical image picked up from old movies. Instead, arriving here, I found myself unpacking in a modern new house, California ranch in design, with palm trees and cactuses in the frontyard. In a way, it was a reassuring sameness.

Perhaps because I had so many unfamiliar things swirling around me, including a new language, the enormous difference between the size and culture of Brobdingnagian L.A. and Lilliputian Lariano wasn't uppermost in my mind. But often, the first thing I heard was: "Los Angeles to Lariano!" The magic of the City of Angels was potent even here, I found.

It altered the way many saw me, but I considered the effect largely a distortion. L.A. is certainly big, powerful and celebrated. It's stressful and challenging, a bewildering and fascinating maze of cultures, subcultures and lifestyles, and cherished home for millions who wouldn't live anywhere else. But it is just a place, I thought, like so many other places. And a place to which I've said goodbye.

It wasn't even a regretful goodbye. When I lived in L.A., I often felt hostile toward the city from being trapped for hours in traffic or being forced to endure the ill-tempered behavior of people with too many differences in the same place at the same time. I echoed common complaints: L.A. sprawls too much, has no architecture to speak of, blah, blah, blah. I was more critic than fan.

One day a few months ago, I decided to write an article about Lariano. I began to look closely at this nondescript village, wondering why its longtime inhabitants love it so. It was then that I understood how completely my everyday perspective is colored and shaped by my memories of Los Angeles, and that those memories are filed in my mind under a powerfully resonating name, *home*. I never see – cannot see – this little town without the warm visual overlay of the enormous city there. And all my previous hissing and booing has transformed into applause.

Writing a description of the single, short and narrow main street that blips through Lariano, I saw the multi-laned L.A. streets extending for miles from downtown to bump into the beaches of Santa Monica, Venice and Malibu. In that same picture were the many rows of tall, skinny palm trees filtering the Southern California sunshine onto the sidewalks and pavement. Lariano sits on the side of a mountain just outside a dense chestnut forest. Here are vistas of the Apennine ranges and of the Mediterranean glimmering far in the distance. As I focused on describing this, pictures of the Los Angeles skyline rose companionably in my mind, daytime and nighttime, the snow-peaked mountaintops of Big Bear on clear days in February, and the intensely colored sunsets so routine on the Pacific horizon.

New images kept announcing their presence: the lassitude of a Sunday afternoon, the air stirred and warmed by Santa Anas; the subtle perfume of desert air; the oddly comforting quiet of ordinary neighborhoods in the Valley, especially in the months when the temperature rises above 100 degrees; the broad, broad beaches, spreading north and south along the South Bay and Malibu coastlines; and so many freeways, always there, always near, always offering escapes to other places.

From more than 6,000 miles away, Los Angeles turns its poetic face to me. Now my mind is filled with sweet reflections; they are neither happy nor sad, just immediate and powerful. The life editor within looks back in wonder at this big, incomprehensible city and deletes the dull and annoying.

It feels redundant to mention how famous Los Angeles is across the planet. Other great cities find fame as places of extraordinary beauty, architecture, history or culture, qualities that Los Angeles shares in varying degrees. But L.A. is singular: Films and television have made it a ubiquitous presence, either as foreground or background. Los Angeles has become the world's hometown. Millions who have never been there consider it familiar. It is luminous in global culture. Angelenos may take it for granted, but it knows its own grandeur. And when you say you're from there, some of its stellar light falls onto you.

Originally published in *The Los Angeles Times Magazine* (March 20, 2005)

2

Odd twists and turns
of new phrases

One of the most frustrating aspects of having inadequate skills in a new language is losing the use of idioms. I miss them almost as if they were boring but cherished longtime companions who have gone away.

I admit that I didn't say "it's raining cats and dogs," for example, all that often back in southern California. But the idiom's familiar presence was always hovering in the background, available. Coming in out of a downpour here in southern Italy, however, if I try a literal Italian translation of the saying I provoke only stares of consternation. To express the same idea in idiomatic Italian, I must say instead, "it's raining as if God sent it." Not bad, really; I like it. It has the gist. But for me, the nonnative speaker, the saying arrived only yesterday. The reflexiveness integral to any true idiom may never arrive for me.

Now approaching the third anniversary of my move here after I married a native Italian, I can describe my progress toward fluency in the complex grammar and gradations of this language and its umpteen dozen dialects as "piano, piano" – to use a popular expression for our "slowly, step by step." My progress is far too "piano," in my opinion, but it's certainly better than it was in my early days here.

I remember just a few months after I arrived when we went to the birthday party of the young daughter of a friend. I had recently enrolled in a beginning Italian class at a school in Rome. The class was four hours a day, four days a week. I was eager to test my progress, though it was meager.

When the pretty little birthday girl dutifully presented herself for introduction, politely kissing me on both cheeks, I took a deep breath and told her my name and asked hers.

A dead pause followed. By the confused look on her face, it was clear I wasn't speaking any kind of Italian she recognized. My husband quickly came to the rescue, repeated what to my ears sounded almost identical to what I had just said and all was well again.

It's the pronunciation, of course. Italian, with its fully sounded vowels and double consonants (also pronounced), is not only a challenge to American speakers, but also a challenge to our untrained ears. It's an audio mystery. The double consonant was a complete surprise to me. We certainly have them in English, but who bothers? In Italian, it's most important to bother or you'll risk disaster.

My own minor calamity occurred while I sent my soon-to-be husband an e-mail for New Year's soon after we met. I intended to wish him a Happy New Year using the Italian expression "*Buon Anno*!" after consulting with an American friend who knew some Italian phrases, I carelessly ignored my recently purchased bilingual dictionary, glowingly typed "*Buon Ano*!" and hit the "send" button. Only afterward did I learn that my friend had neglected the double consonant in her pronunciation and that I had sent greetings to my beloved for a "happy bottom"!

This pronunciation dilemma is a two-way street. The complaint I hear most frequently from the many Italians I meet who have spent years in school studying English is the impossibility of their understanding anything Americans say when we speak to them.

This is true for all languages to some extent, of course. But from what I hear, the offense is especially egregious in American-style English. We engage in a kind of mushing when we enunciate. More accurately, we don't enunciate, which eliminates intelligibility for the nonnative speaker. This is especially true for an Italian, accustomed as he is to a more musical rhythm in language.

How disappointed my husband was one day when he pointed to a roadside area near our home and said "Aye you ka leap toose" and I stared at him blankly. I neither recognized the word "eucalyptus" nor the trees lining the roadway.

Returning to the lost idioms: Although I do mildly mourn their absence, I enjoy discovering the variety in this linguistic area. Sometimes comparable idioms are similar, with perhaps only a change in body part separating them. For example, where we say, "you're pulling my leg," the Italians say, "you're pulling my nose." And instead of "we'll cross that bridge when we come to it," the Italians admonish "not to bandage one's head before breaking it."

For anyone who loves language and imagery, though, the real pleasure occurs when the idiom expresses the same idea but structures the concept in a different way. Take the Italian version of our cryptic "looks count." Choosing personification and lending more majesty to the expression, the Italians say "*vero è che l'occhio vuole la sua parte*," translated literally, "it is true that the eye wants its share."

Learning a second language to the level of fluency is, for me, sheer hard work. But I'm not such a nincompoop that I don't appreciate the privilege of the task and its benefits. It gives me a greatly expanded view and experience of language, its origins and structure. It also helps me see my own language in a fresh light and with greater appreciation.

Observing the reactions of some Italian friends recently after I told them the "cats and dogs" idiom – and watching as they laughed and mimed to each other the incomprehensible experience of being pelted by cats and dogs falling from the sky – brought the saying to life for me for the first time. I still can't use it here and be understood, but then nothing's perfect.

Or, as the Italians say, "*la perfezione non è di questo mondo*" - perfection is not of this world. There's that Italian majesty again.

Originally published in *The Christian Science Monitor* (May 14, 2004)

3

Going to the movies,
Italian style

I still remember the sense of shock I felt. It was about six months after I came to live in Italy. I'm talking to Franco about films I like. Nostalgic about these old movies, and pining for one of LA's ubiquitous mega-sized video stores crammed with Hollywood classics, I mention a famous John Wayne picture. Franco nods in agreement, smiling. He too has seen it.

My sentimental basking in this shared moment of popular culture is abruptly shattered by a suspicion rising tremulously in my mind. "But in English," I say to him, you saw it in English?" No, he says, his John Wayne movies were always dubbed. I stare at him as if he's just confessed he's on the FBI's most wanted list. "You've never heard John Wayne's real voice?!" I squeak.

Until this moment, I hadn't known I had such a passion for the Duke's drawl.

Hollywood movies often fill theater listings in Italy just as they do in many places in the world. American films arrive here in new release almost as quickly as they do in the US. The bump in the *strada* is that the soundtracks, by law, must be dubbed into Italian. This mandate is a leftover from the Mussolini years when there was a wide-ranging ban on various uses of foreign languages in Italy. Reportedly, though, over the ensuing decades the majority of the Italian public has remained quite happy with the practice. The reason could be that Italy is especially renown for the exceptionally high quality of its dubbing and for the extraordinary performance level of the dubbing actors. These actors are famous in their own right here.

All this is small comfort, though, if you aren't fluent in the language. My Italian skills are rising but still have a ways to go.

So when new American films appear that I feel I must see on the big screen, rather than waiting for the dvd, the hunt begins for theaters showing *lingua originale (l.o.)*, or more lately the preferred *versione originale (v.o.)* Only three years ago when I first arrived here, the easiest option was the well-known *Nuovo Pasquino*. It's a small, three-screen theater in the Trastevere quarter. For thirty years it has featured original language films only, many from the USA or Britain.

It was at *Nuovo Pasquino* that I saw some of the *Harry Potter* films and the *Lord of The Rings* trilogy. It's also where I first encountered the Italian custom of stopping the movie midway through for a five-minute break. I remember feeling startled when the soundtrack suddenly gurgled into silence and the image melted chaotically from the screen. Turning to Franco, I said, "Oh, it's broken!"

Instead I learned that this five-minute *bella pausa* is a longstanding gesture of kindness for the bodily needs of simple mortals. Surprisingly, I quickly became accustomed to the short break. I'm especially fascinated by the projectionists' strict adherence to the clock in regulating the pause rather than any well-chosen point in the plot line.

Earlier this year, we decide to drive into Rome to see the last of the *Rings'* trio. Going on line to a popular Italian cinema website to search for an English version of the film, I find the options have expanded. Clicking on the box for original language versions, nine choices for English language films at seven different theaters pop up.

The newest is a multi-screen theater at *Piazza della Repubblica*, next door to Termini, Rome's central train station. The multiplex regularly features popular new releases and, depending on what's currently playing, sometimes offers films in English almost daily (sorry, no bathroom breaks here).

When we arrive at the theater box office, though, we're surprised to find that the 5:30 showing is already sold out. Passing through the crowd outside the theater, I hear enough grumbling English voices to realize more than a few others are similarly surprised.

Still, the advantage to being turned away at a box office when you're in Rome is that... you're in Rome! As we stand nursing our disappointment under the massive portico that runs in front of the theater, our spirits lift quickly. At the heart of the great square in front of us is the mesmerizing *Naiadi* fountain. Under the late afternoon sun its waters sparkle, shooting high and splashing down over the four bronze nymphs decorating its perimeter. And beyond, a half hour's walking in any direction, is Rome's embarrassment of ancient riches – the Pantheon, the Coliseum, the Forum ruins, the Trevi Fountain, the Spanish Steps, Michelangelo's *Piazza del Campidoglio* and, well, you get the idea.

Wandering down the steps from the theater and into the piazza, we decide on a consolation stop at a nearby caffè for a wintertime Italian favorite, hot chocolate rich and thick as pudding, topped with fresh whipped cream. There we mull over the inviting possibilities before us. Shall we search for another movie at one of the other theaters on our list, or shall we just spend the evening wandering through the ancient city?

Without too much struggle, we chose the latter.

April 2004

4

In Italy nothing beats local

Not long ago we were in Rome for a panel discussion open to the public at a local university. The panel topic was international news coverage, and the four guests on the panel were either journalists or scholars. All were from middle eastern countries.

Before the discussion began, each panel member introduced himself to the audience of approximately three hundred people.

The most western in behavior and appearance of the panel members had studied at universities in the US and England, and was fluent in English. On this occasion, however, he spoke in his native language which was simultaneously translated into Italian for the Rome-area audience. The man, a university professor, offered a short bio, and ran through a short list of books he'd written on international affairs.

Then, smiling warmly at the audience, he noted that he had visited Italy several times. He had come often to Rome, he said, and had also traveled to other Italian cities. He mentioned Milan and Florence, and added, "and the most beautiful of all, Venice."

Immediately I heard a barely perceptible, definitely disgruntled sound ripple through the audience. Unaware of his minor blunder, the speaker didn't notice the reaction. I smiled in sympathy. I well recognized his misstep for I had stumbled so myself in my early days in Italy.

Unlearning Yankee ways

It has to do with local pride. In Italy, I found that this home-town loyalty is an often uncompromising and shining force in the culture. So much so that to say to an audience of *Romani* (Rome residents), that Venice (or any other Italian city) is the most beautiful, is received as a mild insult. Just as it would be if the speaker were in Venice and so lauded Rome to the Venetians, or were in Florence, or Naples or Verona or Turin and did the same.

In the first year or so after I came to live here in 2001, we often traveled around Italy. Almost every weekend we were off on a day trip or a couple of nights away, not to mention the annual vacation holidays. Franco loves traveling and he enjoyed showing me the innumerable beautiful places of his country.

Back from a trip, when we visited friends who were our neighbors, I happily prattled away about what we had seen. I praised the sights, and especially the food and wine we had enjoyed. Even with my still meager skills in Italian, it was obvious to me that the response to my elegies was muted. It was puzzling. After all, this was their country and its amazing wonders that I was describing. Why weren't our friends more pleased when I sang Italy's praises?

One day I asked Franco about it and he helped me understand. It turned out to be a classic case of being in Rome but not doing what the Romans do. In fact, I was behaving as if I were in my own country. To praise Miami to someone who lives in Chicago, or to rave about San Francisco to a native of Philadelphia, for example, is perfectly acceptable, even expected back home. It's all America the beautiful, so to speak. It's our national identity that's the strongest, for the most part. An exception is the classic East coast-West coast rivalry of New York versus Los Angeles, but even that seems more playful than serious.

Here in Italy, when I saw our neighbors and praised the Gorgonzola cheese of a city we had just visited, the response was a chorus of praise for the regionally-famous bread of our own small town. And when I raved about the *cucina Toscana* we had enjoyed on a recent weekend in Tuscany, it was greeted with an immediate mention of the porcini mushrooms that grow wild and plentiful in the chestnut forests near where we lived.

So eventually I understood. And, as the Romans and most other Italians do, now when I speak of somewhere we have visited, I adopt the mildly detached tone and measured words that are suitable for such conversation. One in which it's okay to praise the other, but not too much.

Finding home away from home

Which brings to mind one of my favorite memories of when my in-laws came to visit us a few years ago. My father-in-law Bruno is a native of northern Italy. He grew up in a mountain valley in the province of Trentino. His loyalty to his home turf is especially fierce. Bruno and my mother-in-law Sara are both excellent cooks. Meals are planned and prepared with care and close attention to quality of ingredients and flavor of the dishes. Bruno also keeps a good store of his favorite local wines.

During the visit to our home, my father-in-law went along with Franco to the supermarket one day to shop for dinner. I knew that Bruno doesn't generally enjoy traveling, and I was worrying a bit that we needed to do more to make him feel comfortable. So I was surprised when they returned and I saw that he was smiling and seemed more content. I soon saw why. Placing one of the shopping bags on the table, Bruno happily unpacked a half dozen bottles of Trentino wine that he had searched for and found on our local store shelves.

If you read much travel writing, chronicles from centuries ago to present day, it's not unusual to find the writer – whether Dickens or Goethe or an ordinary diarist – puzzling about the key to the particular pleasures of Italian life and the Italian people. *What is it exactly*, is the question explored as the travelers search for the answer.

I'm still searching for that key myself. But possibly it has something to do with this first allegiance of so many Italians to what's local, this love for the thing that is closest, most familiar, and most treasured.

Originally published on *foreignremarks.com* (February 2008)

5

Roberto Benigni:
Speaking in second

Yesterday, while skipping around the Internet in search of one thing, I came across another even better. It was a 1998 interview with Italian actor-writer-director Roberto Benigni, from the UK newspaper *The Guardian*. The previous year Benigni's film *Life is Beautiful* had won three Academy Awards.

Benigni did the interview, which was in front of an audience, entirely in English. At one point in the lengthy and complex discussion, he mentioned that he thought he was being brave in doing the thing in English. Only someone who has never faced such a challenge would disagree with him.

And only someone who has never heard this extraordinarily intelligent man speak wittily and brilliantly in his own native Italian language can understand what a humble and courageous act this was for him.

Six years ago I wouldn't have realized this. Almost certainly I would have felt myself somehow superior to Benigni as I heard the minor errors he made in grammar or pronunciation. Six years ago I was still living in the *blissful* and ignorant world of a monolinguist.

At this point, I want to clarify that I'm not indulging here in a typical bashing of those whose only language is English. In their defense, it is the language that has become the world's lingua franca, for now anyway. So there's no imperative, in a strictly practical sense, for this language population to learn an additional language. And that puts these fellow human beings at a great disadvantage in terms of learning. It's wellknown that the human brain typically enjoys a turbo boost in performance when confronted with true tasks of survival.

You would think by what some say, I mean, that learning a new language is as simple as flipping open a cookbook and following a recipe to bake a cake. Well, for many of us, it *ain't*. It takes a whopping amount of time and effort, and it's often annoying – at times as maddening as it would be if you had to learn how to tie your shoes all over again, only multiply the challenge by a thousand squared. And then there's the simple humiliation when some yahoo snickers at you.

In the past six years I've spent far more time studying to try and master Italian than I would have liked. And I still haven't done it. If it weren't the imperative that it is, given that I live where I do, I would have thrown in the *asciugamano*

How to Live in Italy

early on. All that said, though, it's undeniable that the process of becoming bi-lingual has been deeply beneficial to my own character and global perspective. It's also given me a greater knowledge and appreciation of my mother-tongue that couldn't have been gained any other way.

Looking back, I can see that my preparation for this linguistic challenge began decades ago. A close friend of mine married a man newly arrived in the US from Germany. At that time, I confess, it was I who played the role of snickering yahoo. Imprisoned in my monolingual ghetto, I often teased Michael – who was fluent in English and taught it in a public high school – when he would pronounce a word slightly differently from the native version. He was amazingly good-humored about it, although with hindsight I prefer not to think what he must have felt and thought privately.

The next step in my preparation came years later. I taught English as a Second Language (ESL) for five years in an adult school in Los Angeles. Still hermetically sealed in my one-language world, I rather smugly taught my native language to students from around the world. Bit by bit, though, I became aware of my own provencialism and I also finally awakened to see the challenges second language speakers face.

From that newly born sympathy, I sometimes would tell my students a joke I had read in a textbook: "What do you call someone who speaks three languages? *Tri-lingual*. What do you call someone who speaks two languages? *Bi-lingual*. And what do you call someone who speaks only one language? *American*."

Yes, I know, that's getting close to the bashing I denied earlier but *facts is facts*, as the grammarian said. And I myself was the butt of the joke. More to the point, the struggling students greatly appreciated and needed the empathy.

As the final stage in my language-sensitivity training, life in its sometimes mercurial way swept me off to live in a faraway place where I myself became a second language speaker. Didn't someone once say that Lady justice serves up a fine dish?

And so to my old friend's husband Michael, most belatedly, I want to say I don't mind at all if you enjoy hearing how I've had my comeuppance. And I do apologize! *Colpa mia*!

Originally published on *foreignremarks.com* (January 2007)

6

A Whatchamacallit
by any other name

Standing on the sidewalk in the center of the small Italian town where we live, I was speaking to Franco on the cellphone. He was waiting for me a few blocks away in the car because he had been unable to find parking on the crowded main street. He also was double parked. In that moment I wasn't privy to either of these details.

"What?" he repeated, the decibel level alerting me that he wasn't as joyful as I prefer him to be. "What are you saying?"

"I forgot a part of my glasses," I repeated, covering my free ear to shut out the din of traffic. "The thing that goes over your ears. The handle," I finally mumbled without conviction.

"What? I can't hear you." Decibel level higher. Franco is fluent in English but it was the end of a long day of Saturday shopping. The ambient noise wasn't helping.

"Uh, the thing on the side, you know," I said, knowing that he didn't. "The thing." On the other end, there was a kind of exasperated splutter followed by a mild, definitely non-English expletive, and then silence. You can only push an Italian temperament so far.

Ten minutes earlier I had gone into a local shop to have my reading glasses repaired. The thing, the handle, the whatever – that part of the glasses I now knew I didn't know the name of in any language – had fallen off. When I opened my glasses case for the shop assistant, however, I realized I had neglected to bring along the detached part.

Minutes later, Franco pulled up in the car and I climbed in. I avoided the laser-like gaze turned in my direction. "What is the Italian word for those things on our glasses that go over our ears?" I asked, in exasperation.

"*Stanghetta*," he said, with the ringing confidence of a descendant of Imperial Rome.

"Ah. I don't think we have a word for that in English," I said, even though I sensed this wasn't the time to compare and contrast languages.

The drive home was rather quiet.

Some days later, the glasses fixed, I sat down at my computer. My mission was to track down the word that had eluded me the previous Saturday. After checking several sites, including Encarta, Wikipedia, an Indiana University library page, and other information and opticians' sites, I had collected a good sampling.

The term I myself had mumbled, the humble "handle," popped up often, I found. "Arm" and "leg" also are popular. Inelegant, it seemed to me, but at least they were familiar vocabulary. It was on the scholarly and historical sites that I faced strange stuff. There I first spotted the alarming "rigid sidepieces." I rehearsed this new lexicon, re-visioning my cellphone conversation with Franco: "I forgot one of my rigid sidepieces." Oh yes, that certainly would have worked!

Finally, I unearthed what seems to be an official choice. "Temples." The nomenclature of opticians. In my memory I returned to the noisy weekend sidewalk, shouting into the cellphone, "I forgot one of my temples." I probably would have had to walk home.

I did uncover some stray facts. Many now agree that eyeglasses were invented in Italy in the 1200s, although England's Sir Francis Bacon also gets a nod. But the Italians only invented the lens. They sat precariously via a bridge on the nose, or were mounted in a frame, as with the monocle. There weren't any handles-legs-arms-rigid sidepieces-temples-whatever. That ingenuity didn't occur until the 1700s. It is attributed to an Englishman, Edward Scarlett.

Once I learned of Mr. Scarlett, I decided to deepen my inquiry by checking in with a British friend. Perhaps, being the inventor of the you-know-what, the English might have the authoritative word for them. Perhaps it just never made it across the Atlantic to the colonies. I picked up the phone.

"Hi Lesley, an odd question, but what do you call those things on a pair of eyeglasses that sit on either side of our heads?"

"Arms," Lesley said promptly. "Or sides. Darling," (talking to her husband, not me), "what do you call the sides of eyeglasses?"

I heard darling say confidently, "Arms."

"Yes," Lesley said, to me again, "yes, arms, I think." A pause and then she continued confidently. "Opticians would say spectacle sides. Or they might refer to them as frame sidepieces... or frame sides... interesting." Less confidently, "I don't know, really. They don't call them ear sides... yes, arms is the most common reference in England."

And some say the United States and England are two countries separated by a common language![1]

Originally published on *foreignremarks.com* (April 2007)

---

[1] *England and America are two countries separated by a common language.* (George Bernard Shaw)

How to Live in Italy

7

Book review

Mouse or Rat?
TRANSLATION AS NEGOTIATION
by Umberto Eco

What am I missing? is the worrying question that often can arise for the curious reader of works in translation. What has been lost in the journey from the words, ideas and literary style of the original work, to the secondary version now before me? Can I trust that the mind and creation of the original author are truly represented in the translation, or am I reading something here that is predominantly reflective of the mind and ideas of the translator?

In *Mouse or Rat? TRANSLATION AS NEGOTIATION*, Umberto Eco reflects on the process of translation. He considers what it is actually possible for the translator to achieve, and specifically how he or she can go about it. In this compact book, Eco writes from the rare perspective of a highly successful author who has had his own work translated into many different languages and who himself has often translated the works of others.

The question of loss in translation is always a major concern. In the second chapter of *Mouse or Rat?*, Eco writes about this. To illustrate how it can happen, he discusses an Italian translation of Herman Melville's *Moby Dick*. Specifically he recounts how the translator dealt with the classic book's famous first line, "Call me Ishmael." Previous Italian translators, he notes, have translated the line in a word-for-word rendering of Melville's, as in *Chiamatemi Ismaele*.

The translator of the version Eco is citing as an exception, Bernardo Draghi, wrote three pages of notes to explain how he himself made the decision to translate the line otherwise. Draghi chose this: *Diciamo che mi chiamo Ismaele* (Let's say that my name is Ishmael). In Draghi's notes, as Eco recounts it:

> Draghi remarks that the original opening line suggests at least three readings: (i) "My real name is not Ishmael, but please call me so, and try to guess what my choice means (think of the fate of Ishmael son of Abraham and Agar)"; (ii) "My name is not important, I am only a witness of a great tragedy"; (iii) "Let us be on first-name terms, take me as a friend, trust my report."

> Now let us assume that Melville really wanted to suggest one or more of those readings, and that there was a reason why he did not write *My name is Ishmael...* Even though I appreciate the rest of this

translation, I cannot but object that (apart from the fact that the Italian version is less concise than the original) with his choice, Draghi has inevitably stressed interpretations (i) and (ii), but has eliminated the third one. In any case, he is warning the Italian reader that, in introducing the character, there is something to discover, while the English reader still remains free to decide whether or not to give particular importance to that expression. It seems to me that this translation says on one side less and on the other side more than the original. More, because it states which one of the possible readings of the original is to be selected, less because – if Melville wanted to remain ambiguous – Draghi eliminates part of the ambiguity.

Eco isn't suggesting, however, that the remedy for loss in translation is for the translator to deliver a word for word *photo-copy* of the original. Even if it were desirable, Eco notes, given the sometimes insurmountable differences in languages, a literal rendition isn't even possible.

Three times in the book, in discussing this challenge of the insurmountable differences in languages, Eco cites the remark by a well-known scholar that "one cannot express in a jungle language a sentence such as *neutrinos lack mass.*"

Another reason such literal reproduction isn't desirable, according to Eco, is that different languages often employ different images, in effect, to say the same thing. As an example, he offers a particular comparison between Italian and English.

Let us suppose that in a novel a character says, *You're just pulling my leg.* To render such an idiom in Italian by *stai solo tirandomi la gamba* or *tu stai menandomi per la gamba* would be literally correct but misleading. In Italian one should say *mi stai prendendo per il naso*, thus substituting an English leg for an Italian nose. If literally translated, the English expression, absolutely unusual in Italian, would make the reader suppose that the character (as well as the author) was inventing a provocative rhetorical figure – which is completely misleading as in English the expression is simply an idiom. By choosing *nose* instead of *leg* a translation puts the Italian reader in the same situation as the original English one. Thus only by being literally *unfaithful* can a translator succeed in being truly faithful to the source text.

Umberto Eco is probably best known to the American public for his own 1983 novel *The Name of the Rose*. The book sold more than ten million copies and was translated into some thirty languages, according to the UK newspaper *The Guardian*. It was also made into a major Hollywood film of the same name.

The 74-year-old Eco is Professor of Semiotics at Bologna University in Italy. He is the author of four other novels, as well as more than twenty-five non-fiction books primarily on the topics of semiotics, linguistics, aesthetics and morality. He has been awarded more than thirty honorary doctorates from prominent universities in various countries. In addition

How to Live in Italy

to his native language, he speaks French, Spanish and German and is also fluent in English.

A final note, if you are reading *Mouse or Rat?* in English, you need not worry about any loss. Eco wrote the book in English.

_____

January 2007

PART TWO

Food, glorious food

You may have the universe if I may have Italy.
Giuseppe Verdi

8

A grape snack

Pizzutello is the name of a white table grape that our neighborhood fruit and vegetable vendor, Felice, describes as *un po' particolare* (a little special). A few days ago, a basket full of grapes was next to his cash register. As he was weighing the various produce I had selected, he plucked some of the grapes off one of the clumps and handed them to me to taste.

"Fifty years ago, it was the custom of farm workers to hold a fistful of these grapes in one hand, and a piece of bread in the other, and eat them together," Felice said. He smiled at my look of disbelief. "Really, they did," he repeated, "you should try it."

As soon as I got home, I sliced off a piece of the freshly baked bread I had just bought and tried the odd culinary duo myself. Although it took me a moment to appreciate, I enjoyed the contrasting tastes, just as Felice had predicted I would.

Pizzutello also is sometimes called *corna* (horn) because of its elongated oval shape. Tivoli, a small town east of Rome, hosts an annual Pizzutello festival each fall, featuring grapes from local vineyards.

The Pizzutello grape is especially valued for its sweetness, and for its resistance to damage in transport, according to experts. Pizzutello also comes in a black (purple) variety.

Originally published on *foreignremarks.com* (October 2007)

9

Bread and water in Apulia

As a waiter arranged the plates of antipasto in front of us, I felt the happy curiosity of discovering a new dish. We had ordered a regional specialty called *friselle pugliesi*. The *friselle* are round, rock hard breads a little bigger than an English muffin. Each serving is accompanied by side dishes of toppings of grilled and fresh vegetables, and with an individual bowl of water, and metal tongs.

Eying the last two items, my eagerness ebbed an inch or so. I ignored this inner advisory, however, and turned my adoring gaze back toward the humble-appearing culinary hero on my plate.

As the waiter turned to go, Franco, mildly perplexed, asked if we could have some how-to tips.

The young man pointed at the bread and the tongs and the bowl of water and suggested we use the middle item to put the first object into the latter.

"But only leave the bread in for about half a minute or it will become too wet and fall apart," he added, with what seemed to me a suspiciously low level of enthusiasm. He moved away quickly.

Just then, another waiter arrived at the table of four next to us. He was carrying dishes piled high with small, freshly baked balls of something, a savory steam wafting upward. "What's that?" I asked Franco, my nose twitching like a hungry piglet's. He shrugged, "I don't know."

I turned back to the granite like object on my own plate.

Where and when

We were sitting at a table in a front corner on the covered terrace of a seaside restaurant in southeast Apulia. It was the end of a pleasantly warm, late June day. The sun had just vanished over the horizon. Waves were lapping, breezes were blowing, *cucina italiana* aromas were wafting. All seemed blissfully promising on this night out one evening during our recent vacation in the southern Italian region Italians call *Puglia* (pronounced pool-yah).

Using the tongs, I placed the bread in the bowl of water and mentally counted off thirty seconds. Then I returned the bread to my plate, I clearly heard a clunk as it landed. So I dunked it back in the water. I waited another thirty seconds, then another. A rock would have been more porous. Hoping for some abracadabra-like magic, I ceased the soaking process. I proceeded to pile the veggies on top of the still rigid ring and began to saw away at it with my knife. In vain. Resting from my labor, I munched on the grilled eggplant, bell peppers, zucchini and fresh chopped tomatoes. They were delicious.

Some time later, an elegant and charming woman came along with the waiter to our table. She had about her an air of solicitude and the authoritative presence of a majordomo or benevolent management. Observing the ragged-edged chunks of bread littering my plate, she smiled down at me with an expression of pitying wisdom.

"I think it takes some experience," I said meekly.

"Yes," she nodded, picking up the plate. I heard her laughing softly as she walked away.

What it is

Friselle, also known as *frise*, are made from an old Apulian recipe using wheat flour that is only partially refined, according to *Wikipedia Italia*. They are baked in the oven, then cut in half horizontally and baked again. The bread's strong point is that it keeps for ages. So it was a practical sack lunch for farm workers and sailors, and sometimes it was the only bread available to the poor during hard times when flour was scarce.

Another local bread

A few days later, exploring the town of Ostuni, we discovered the *friselle*'s opposite in the Apulia bread kingdom. Also a regional specialty, it is *la sfogliata*. For this bread, the dough is folded over a filling, and then fried or baked. More importantly, when you bite into it, you don't crack any molars.

We bought our first one at a local bakery where the irresistible aromas lured us inside. The baker had just pulled a tray full of *sfogliate* from the oven. The filling was a creamy spinach concoction. The bread was moist and flaky in texture, and tasted rich and almost sweet. In a case of the cliché proving true, it actually feels as if it's melting in your mouth.

We ate these *sfogliate* two more times – easily found in coffee bars and bakeries – once again with the creamy spinach filling and on another occasion, with a filling of fresh ricotta and tomato sauce.

Apulians eat well

To avoid being tarred and feathered by any passing *Pugliesi*, as Apulians are called in Italian, for my critique of the proud and stony *friselle*, I must add this tribute to the food of Apulia. The region is renown, along with its southern neighbors Campania and Sicily, for the taste, preparation and quality of its food. Typical dishes are often described as humble and poor but highly nutritious and flavorful.

With a Mediterranean coastline wrapping around much of it, Apulia is, not surprisingly, also known for its fish, especially shellfish. And the Apulia region is Italy's largest producer of wine and olive oil, according to the magazine *La Cucina Italiana*. In recent years, its editors say, Apulia has been gaining a reputation for producing good wines.

Afterword

Two years later, I got an e-mail from a reader protesting my failure to appreciate the *friselle*. She wrote:

> We are Americans living in Puglia. Whoa, did you
> ever miss the boat on the *friselle*. Our Italian friends
> simply hold it under the tap until the desired
> amount of water is absorbed – some like it crunchy,
> but many like it tender.
>
> It is splendid, and serves as the absolutely most
> appropriate palette for the fine oil and fresh
> tomatoes and herbs of the region. We first tried it
> on a sailboat off the coast of Brindisi. Our Captain
> and his lady handed us each a moist *friselle* with
> tomatoes, oil, salt and anchovies. To die for! Try it
> again – keep it simple, eat it with your hands, and
> you'll fall in love."

Originally published on *foreignremarks.com* (July 2007)

10

Caffè Camelia and Rodolfo

Rodolfo Manuini has a theory about why tourism in Chianti has been sinking like a rock for the past few years. The villains he names are not the pricey euro or the shrinking dollar but rather the local businessperson and producer who simply set their prices too high.

As owner of Caffè Camelia in the village of Villa a Sesta in Tuscany he has watched his own business shrivel during this downswing. So he states his thesis with a passion tinged with frustration. He talks first about the sharp drop in Americans vacationing in Europe.

"That was understandable considering the Twin Towers and the war. But the Germans and British also stopped coming," he says, speaking in Italian and shrugging his shoulders in mystification.

Then he offers some evidence for his particular conclusions about greedy merchants.

"Recently I went to a coffee bar in Florence with three of my friends," he says. "We each ordered an aperitif, standing at the serving counter, and we each paid 4.50 euro. Standing!" he reiterates, alluding to the Italian custom of caffè owners often charging double for items served at a table rather than at the bar.

"As a bar owner myself, I know the basic cost of an aperitif is only fifty cents. Even taking into account taxes, other expenses and a reasonable profit margin, you should only charge the customer two euro maximum."

There are still people around who have money to spend, he says, and the piazzas are still full of tourists on weekends and holidays. But from what he is observing, he says, those on more limited budgets are beginning to go to the local supermarket and buying a panino instead of going to restaurants.

The situation got so bad that Rodolfo removed the locally-produced Chianti wine from his menu for a while. With his entrees moderately priced at an average of eight euro, Rodolfo's customers weren't buying the expensive bottles of Chianti, Rodolfo says. They simply chose something cheaper. One day the local producer came to see him and asked him why he was no longer serving his wine. Hearing that it cost too much, the businessman agreed to lower his prices, and Rodolfo began offering the wine to his patrons again.

This is our second visit to Caffè Camelia. It's in the center of its tiny village dating back to the Etruscan age (700 BC) in the Italian district of Chianti. The geographical district sprawls broadly over central Tuscany. It is, perhaps, best known as home to the massively-popular, medieval town of Siena.

The area surrounding Villa a Sesta is a tranquil sweep of low hills, intertwining of four rivers, woodland of oak, chestnut trees, and cypresses, and vineyards and olive groves.

There are only forty-five people on average per square kilometer in the local county, according to official statistics. These lucky souls live among a scattering of beautifully preserved middle-age villages, adjoined by a countryside of castles, villas, 12th century farmhouses, ancient monasteries and churches. When the sun shines down on a warm, breeze filled day on this privileged spot on the planet, it can bring a balm to the human spirit unmatched by most anything.

I could claim it was mainly this that drew me back to Villa a Sesta. But, to be honest, it was a culinary vision that lured me – the memory of the *crostoni* that Rodolfo offers as an antipasto. On our first visit, a couple of years earlier, I saw it served to another customer. I almost whimpered with envy as I saw the hot, melted, freshly grated pecorino cheese thickly glopped over half-inch-thick slices of homemade Tuscan bread. I turned for comfort to my own order of bruschetta, the bread brushed with garlic and loaded with mounds of chopped fresh tomatoes and fresh basil sprinkled with olive oil. But even as I munched away on the delicious combo, my gaze kept turning covetously toward the dish I hadn't ordered.

I vowed to return and now on a rainy, windy day in early April we have. Beginning with antipasto of the *crostoni*, we are now on the second course. My choice is handmade tagliatelle with a ragu sauce of *cinghiale* (wild boar). A bottle of local Chianti (12 euro) is at center table, already half-empty.

Owing to the wet weather probably, the village and cafe are almost deserted. Rodolfo, genial as before, has time for conversation.

A former maitre d'hotel, Rodolfo says his wife, Artchara, bought Caffè Camelia in 2001. Previously it was owned by the Camelia family who have another restaurant, the Michelin-starred *Bottega del 30*, only about 50 yards away. Artchara, who is from Thailand and holds a master's degree in economics, was then a cook at the cafe. When the Camelia family decided to sell it, she snapped it up.

The Camelias are celebrated master chefs specializing in traditional and ancient Tuscan cuisine. Working alongside them, Artchara learned her culinary skills well. Two other dishes on the menu, for example – which already have me plotting another trip back – are spaghetti *alla chitarra* with grated pecorino cheese, red pepper and parsley, and gnocchi with gorgonzola.

As during our first visit, Rodolfo still speaks unhappily of the slowdown of tourism to Chianti in recent years. He describes how producers of Chianti Classico, the region's star wine, have watched their cantinas fill up with unsold stock as demand has fallen. Rodolfo sticks with his earlier hypothesis about inflated prices as the primary problem. Now, he says, some of the producers are also seeing this.

How to Live in Italy

They've lowered their prices, he says, and sales are beginning to pick up again. He's hoping with the return of the sun this spring, an uptrend also will come back to tourism, and he will see a line of customers pushing through his door.

April 2005

11

Calabria and the elusive eggplant

It was mid-June last year when we made the six-hour drive south from Rome to the Crotone area of the Calabria. The region of Calabria is at the southern tip of Italy, nose to nose with the island of Sicily. The website for the beach area, vacation apartment we had booked promised breakfast every day, and a once-a-week special dinner featuring *melanzana ripiena* (stuffed eggplant).

As it happened, this special dish had become a focal point of our Calabria visit. I first heard of it when I mentioned our upcoming trip to a friend who grew up nearby.

"Oh, you must have their *melanzana ripiena!*" (melon-zah-nah ree-pea-aye-nah) she said, touching her cheek with her index finger in the classic Italian gesture for praising delicious food.

From that moment, my images of spending lazy, sunny days on the beaches winding along the Mediterranean coastline there were mingled with visions of tasting the eggplant specialty. The plan also included dropping by a local restaurant or two and sampling the same dish from their menus.

But I neglected to read the fine print in the tourist brochure. While checking in at the front office of the vacation residence, we learned that the breakfasts and special dinners are only offered during high season. That would be the sweltering months of July and August when millions of Italians head for the cooling breezes of the seaside.

Many of the local restaurants also don't open their doors until July, we found. We did find a busy restaurant nearby that served lots of local fresh seafood, swordfish in particular. But no eggplant was on the menu, stuffed or otherwise.

Finding eggplant on planet earth usually isn't so difficult. Though housed in the vegetable section of supermarkets, the plump purple eggplant is, botanically speaking, a berry. It's grown in lots of places around the world. This includes Asia, its native home, the Middle East and various Western countries.

According to experts, the fruit thrives best when grown in tropical and sub-tropical climates. Calabria, is especially ideal for eggplant, these same experts say, because of the region's dryness. In summer the temperatures soar, and the soil is almost free of calcium. For the eggplant, this combination of factors keep the level of bitter juices in the fruit low and deepen the sweet flavor.

The *Calabresi*, as the locals are called, have as many as eighty different recipes featuring eggplant as the main ingredient, according to one local writer.

My ambition to sample this regional star, however, was also foiled by the calendar. Eggplant harvest in Calabria isn't until August. What saved the day was an invitation that, at the time, I had no idea would bring me any closer to this elusive berry masquerading as a vegetable. The father of the proprietor of the vacation residence where we were staying, Don Franco, seemed to especially enjoy having the opportunity to talk to English speaking guests. His wife is British and he himself is fluent.

Semi-retired, and gregarious by nature, he appears very much at home mingling with the guests and making sure everyone is comfortable. In the warm evenings, he could usually be seen somewhere along the row of private front terraces of the apartments offering advice about favorite tourist spots or answering questions.

He offered us various guidebooks and maps for day trips to nearby areas. One day he even acted as a personal guide to some nearby ruins of a Roman villa. Included was a stopover at the farm of a local shepherd where we got to see the family making its daily production of fresh ricotta cheese that is sold in local markets.

As a thank you to Don Franco, we invited him to an al fresco dinner on our terrace the next evening. He happily accepted (his wife was away on a trip to England). We did find it curious that he made a point of insisting on bringing the *vegetables* for the meal.

And that's how I finally got to taste Calabria's celebrated eggplant dish. When Don Franco arrived he was accompanied by a longtime neighbor Caterina. Having heard my disappointment about the elusive eggplant, he had asked Caterina to make a dish of *melanzana ripiena* just for us. She delivered it to our table, warm and fresh from the oven.

And, of course, when we asked she gave us the recipe.

Melanzana ripiena (for four people)

Ingredients:
  tomato sauce
  2 medium to large eggplants
  1/2 lb ground beef
  2 cups fresh bread crumbs (Italian or French bread, torn
      into small pieces)
  1 medium to large clove garlic, minced
  1 small onion, finely chopped or sliced
  one egg
  2 tbsp olive oil
  1/2 glass white wine
  1 cube vegetable bouillon (no msg)
  1/2 cup fresh parmesan cheese, roughly grated
  1/2 cup fresh cheese, roughly grated or thinly sliced
      (provolone, grana padano or other)

Preheat oven to 350 degrees. Slice eggplant in two lengthwise and, using a spoon, scoop out the pulp and put in a small bowl. Set pulp aside. In a separate pan, bring two cups of water to boil, add 1/2 tsp. salt. Add the eggplant pulp to the boiling water and continue to boil for three minutes. Drain the cooked pulp and squeeze out excess water. Set aside. In a large saute pan, heat the olive oil, and then add the garlic and onion. Cook over medium heat for two minutes, being careful not to burn the mixture. Add the ground beef and, stirring as needed, cook for five minutes. Add the wine, and continue cooking until the wine evaporates, stirring as needed. Add bouillon, 1/3 of the tomato sauce, and cook at a low simmer for five more minutes. Remove this meat mixture from the fire and allow to cool. When the meat mixture has cooled, add the breadcrumbs, the eggplant pulp, the Parmesan cheese and the egg. Mix well together.

In a baking pan, spread half of the remaining tomato sauce in the bottom. Place the four halves of the eggplant in the baking pan, bottom sides down, and brush the insides lightly with olive oil. Spread the remaining 1/2 cup of cheese in the bottom of the eggplant sections, dividing equally. Now fill the eggplant sections with the meat mixture. Pour the remaining tomato sauce evenly over the meat layer. Put in the oven for twenty to thirty minutes (until the eggplant is cooked). Serve warm.

June 2008

12

Nuts about Nocino

"Would you ask Pina if I could have some *noci?*" Franco called to me as I picked up the phone.

He was using the Italian word for nuts, and, in this case, referring specifically to green, unripened walnuts. Pina and her husband Romano are friends from the small country town where we lived until recently. When we visit, they often give us fruits and vegetables from their overflowing gardens and various orchards.

"Oh, you're going to make some more nocino," I said, pleased.

Nocino is one of Italy's many digestives – those potent alcoholic confections that quickly soothe a stomach upset by an incoming tide of too much of what's too good from the Italian table. These aids to digestion are generally made from a base of ingredients including a variety of herbs, spices or fruits. These are combined with high grade alcohol and, sometimes, sugar. In nocino, nuts are the indispensable ingredient.

A wellknown Italian digestive is limoncello, best served ice cold. We keep ours in the freezer compartment. Other digestives are of a wide variety and are often simply referred to as *amari*, or in English, bitters. Two that we have in our home collection are *Fernet Branca* and *Strega*.

My favorite digestive, however, is the lesser-known nocino. It has a rich, sweet taste. Nocino isn't so easy to find in bars or supermarkets, so we sometimes make our own. Or more precisely, Franco makes it and I drink it. Rather than nocino, he prefers that Italian superstar, grappa, a liqueur so powerful it would elicit a gasp from a rhinoceros.

Wellknown grappa brands include *Nonino*, and Franco's personal favorites, *Nardini* and *Bertagnolli*.

Discovering Nocino

The first time I tasted nocino was a few months after I arrived in Italy. One evening, after returning from dinner with some friends, I was suffering the usual penalty for gluttony, a mildly upset stomach. I resigned myself to hours of the inevitable discomfort.

One of our wedding gifts was a bottle of homemade nocino. Up to that moment, it had been residing in the back of a kitchen cupboard, its pretty artisanal bottle unopened. Hearing my Eeyore like grumblings, Franco suggested I try some nocino, assuring me it would help. I scowled, expressed my doubts, but consented to give it a try. The taste was delicious, and shortly thereafter my indigestion had disappeared. To this day, I'm still amazed at the seemingly magical healing effect of a few tablespoons of something so simple.

Below is the recipe we use, as given to us by Romano.

Nocino by Romano

Ingredients:

   18 green (unripe) whole walnuts still in their rinds
   1 quart alcohol – 190 proof (95%)
   1 tablespoon cinnamon
   1 tablespoon cloves
   12 ounces sugar
   1 quart water

Important tip: according to folk tradition, the walnuts should be picked on *giorno di San Giovanni* (St. John's Day, June 24).

Cut each nut (rind and all) into eight pieces (hint: definitely wear gloves to prevent dark stains to skin). Put the alcohol, the nut pieces, the cinnamon and the cloves into a large jar that has a lid. Set the jar in a dark place and leave it for approximately forty days. When this time has elapsed, strain the nuts and alcohol mixture into another container. Discard the nut residue, and set the container of liquid aside.

Bring the water to a boil for five minutes, then remove from heat. Add the sugar to the water and stir until dissolved. Let this sugar mixture cool completely and then pour it into the nut alcohol mixture. Pour this combined liquid into a pretty bottle, and make a label. The nocino is ready to serve.

Originally published on *foreignremarks.com* (June 2007)

13

The Cook, the Sauce, the Critic, and the Grim Finale

Not long ago, I wandered into the kitchen and, opening the door to the refrigerator, meditated on the contents. Gazing at the carrots and bell peppers, I ruminated on life's injustices. It was a Sunday night and in our shared schedule of kitchen duty, Franco usually cooks on weekends. But he was hunched over his laptop, engrossed in some bring-home work project. I had surrendered to the realization that if we were going to eat before the wee hours, I would have to do the cooking.

Earlier in the day we talked about making a pasta with Franco's special anchovy sauce, one of his favorites. It's a dish with a subtle, mellow flavor, without any of the overpowering punch this tiny pungent fish usually delivers. The thing was, I hadn't a clue how to make the sauce.

The Sauce

Bravely, I reached to the top refrigerator shelf and took out the covered dish containing the fish. There were about a half dozen salted, whole ones that we had bought recently. I selected one and set it aside on the cutting board. Next I opened the vegetable drawer and took out a head of fresh broccoli.

I had decided to create my own anchovy sauce. (Warning: good cooks might find the following painful) First I chopped a small onion and minced some garlic. I put a couple of tablespoons of olive oil in a sauté pan, added the onion and set the flame to low. After a few minutes, I added the garlic and cooked it all for another minute.

After washing the broccoli, I cut off the florets and added them to the onion-garlic mixture.

I added a half a cup of canned tomatoes, a little water, salt and pepper, and set the flame to high.

I turned my attention to the single small fish I had selected. I chopped it into tiny pieces and added these to the sauce.

I covered the sauté pan and let the sauce cook on the medium high flame for a half an hour, adding water as needed to prevent the sauce from burning. In the meantime, I boiled some water for the pasta, added a couple of tablespoons of salt, and some number five spaghetti. When the pasta was done, I was also ready to add the final ingredient for the sauce. Turning off the flame under the sauté pan, I added a few tablespoons of panna (thick cream) to the pan, stirring it to blend with the cooked broccoli and fish mixture.

How to Live in Italy

In the meantime I had set the table and poured the wine. I called to Franco that dinner was ready.

The Critic

"How is it," I asked Franco, watching him after he took his first bite. I had already tasted mine but I was reserving judgment.

"Good," Franco said, but in a way that immediately alerted me to troublesome subtext.

"Really? Are you sure."

"It needs pepper."

"I added pepper. Do you mean black pepper or red?"

"Both."

"Oh, well I added black."

A minute more passed.

"It has anchovy in it, you know," I said.

"Really, no, I don't taste it."

"Yes, it does. I can taste it."

Franco poked at the pasta in his plate. "What's are these red pieces?"

I ignored the question and pursued the anchovy theme.

"Can't you taste the anchovy?" I said. "I can."

"No," Franco said, the expression on his face clearly indicating a yearning for the taste eluding him.

"What are these red things?" he asked again, pushing one with his fork.

"Tomato."

"Ah," he said. "The problem with tomato is that it's strong. It has a killing effect on other flavors."

"But I only added half a cup."

We continued eating. It seemed to me Franco's features had taken on the stoical aspect they sometimes do on the days when I cook.

The Grim Finale

"How do you make your sauce?" I asked.

"The ingredients are the salt preserved fish, two for each person, olive oil, two tablespoons for each person, garlic, a half to one clove for each person, parsley and red pepper."

"Uh huh."

"First you clean the fish. Take off the extra salt then cut them open longitudinally. Take off the spine, tail and extra interior stuff. In a skillet, on very low heat, pour olive oil. Add the fish, minced garlic, minced parsley and let it stay until the fish meat is dissolved."

"Do you mean you're supposed to do all that stuff you said to the fish before you cook them?"

"Yes, while the water is boiling for the pasta, you clean the fish."

"Oh. I just chopped one up."

"And the bones?"

"Uh huh, I put everything into the sauce."

Lengthy pause.

"Are you confusing oil anchovies with salted sardines?" Franco asked. A veritable dawn of illumination was crossing his face.

"Salted sardines?" I echoed faintly.

"The ones we bought a few days ago, and that I put in the glass dish on the top shelf of the refrigerator."

At least I know now why he couldn't taste the anchovies.

Originally published on *foreignremarks.com* (August 2007)

14

The birthplace of Gorgonzola.
Maybe.

GORGONZOLA, ITALY – Ever since someone told me a few years ago that there is a town in northern Italy named Gorgonzola, and that the townspeople, the *Gorgonzolesi*, claim that their ancestors created the famous cheese of the same name, I have wanted to go there to find out if the proof is in the pudding – or in this case, the curd.

In short, is the Gorgonzola in Gorgonzola really better?

I got my opportunity to find out last September. We arrived there on the second day of the town's autumn fair. The annual three-day festival celebrates the history and development of the rich, creamy cheese.

Meeting us at the metro station, after our half-hour ride from our homebase in downtown Milan, was Enzo Casanova. A friend of a friend, he and his family live in an adjoining town, and he offered to give us an aficionado's tour of Gorgonzola.

I confess I was licking my lips in anticipation of the taste tour that I was sure was awaiting us.

This was the moment I learned that no Gorgonzola is made in Gorgonzola anymore. One reason, Enzo pointed out, is that the town has been absorbed into the greater Milan metropolitan area and is no longer the big farming area it once was. Instead it's a bedroom community for commuters.

The major cheese producers are now in nearby towns and provinces, and one, Pasturo, even claims that it, rather than Gorgonzola, is the birthplace of the pungent cheese.

One thing Gorgonzola is not relinquishing, however, is its assertion that it is the place to come if you want to see where the namesake cheese was first created. The annual festival is a loud declaration of this.

The Sagra Nazionale del Gorgonzola (*sagra* means festival) takes over the center of the small village. The hub of the celebration is on Via Italia, the town's short main street.

For the first half hour, we wandered along this street, happily accepting free samples of Gorgonzola *dolce* and Gorgonzola *piquant*, served melted or at room temperature on bite-size chunks of bread.

Somewhat satisfied, we followed Enzo as he led us through an adjacent street to another section of the village a few blocks away. Along the way, we passed more booths with various types and brands of Gorgonzola and freshly made breads on sale. Restaurants were also open, with tables and umbrellas set up outside their doors.

Did Leonardo enjoy Gorgonzola?

At the end of the street is the narrow Martesana canal. Admired and studied by Leonardo da Vinci, the canal was built in 1457 and is one of a small network spreading out in various directions from Milan. The canal attracts many visitors to Gorgonzola, Enzo told us, adding that according to local legend, da Vinci also laid out the master plan for the village while he was visiting in the area.

It was just after we crossed the low-arched stone bridge over the canal that we saw the other big star of the fair, Amaranto. She was hustling her 1,500 pounds across her temporary pen toward an admiring crowd of fans. Thrusting her big head through the narrow metal poles of the makeshift fence, she placidly accepted the caresses of the dozens of hands of her fans, her great eyes gazing here and there, thinking only a cow knows what.

A few yards away we met her owner, Emilio Manzoni. A dairy farmer from Gorgonzola, Mr. Manzoni was demonstrating how to make a simple cheese and then distributing small scoops of the freshly made white curd to his audience. "In my opinion, it needs a little sugar and a little salt," one taster said, playing critic. Mr. Manzoni just smiled good-naturedly and continued handing out the samples.

When I asked about Amaranto, he told me she is a Brown Swiss, the ancient breed from the Alps that first provided the milk for making Gorgonzola. Today, he said, cheesemakers prefer another breed, Holstein Friesian, because its milk output is greater.

The birthplace of Gorgonzola. Maybe.

Once upon a cow

But Amaranto and her ancestors still have the place of honor in the legend of how Gorgonzola came to be created, and so Manzoni brings her to the fair for people to see.

Although no official documentation exists of the cheese's birth, its origins are estimated to go as far back as the 13th century or earlier.

In one version of the story, it is said that in those days, herdsmen from the north brought their cows down from the mountains in September to graze on the lush, sweet grass of the plains surrounding Milan. The first stop along the southern migration was the tiny settlement of Gorgonzola. To show their gratitude to the local landowners for the grazing rights, the herdsmen offered them the milk from the herd. It was with this large supply of milk that the *Gorgonzolesi* started to make and sell cheese.

This first cheese was called *stracchino*, from the Italian word meaning "tired." It is a reference to the milk that came from the cows that were exhausted after their long migration south.

The lowly *stracchino's* successor, Gorgonzola, was an accidental invention.

As writer Oriana Morini Casalini recounts it, one evening, a love-struck *casaro*, or cheesemaker, rushed out to meet his girlfriend without finishing his work. The following morning, fearing he might lose his job if it was discovered he had thrown out the previous day's batch of unfinished cheese curd, he surreptitiously dumped it in with the new milk supply.

This set in motion a process that produced a greenish-blue-veined curd with a strange look and a pungent odor – sometimes compared to smelly socks by detractors – and Gorgonzola cheese was born.

We thought about this as we headed home with Enzo and to a dinner, prepared by his wife, Teresa, of pasta with Gorgonzola sauce.

Teresa had recently completed a course in gastronomy offered by La Cucina Italiana and is passionate about food. Now she is using her training as a volunteer at the school her 11-year-old son, Marco, attends. She gives the children lessons in food appreciation and nutrition.

The world's best cheeses

In her small but well-equipped kitchen, as she was preparing the pasta sauce, I asked Teresa if she agreed with the popular notion that France has the best cheeses. The other three Italians sitting nearby immediately and vigorously dissented, but the more food-democratic Teresa agreed that France has excellent cheeses. Italy's cheeses are just as good, however, she said, and more varied.

And her ranking of the top three cheeses in the world? The answer was instantaneous: Parmigiano-Reggiano, grana padano, and Gorgonzola.

All Italian, of course.

Teresa's Mezzani With Walnuts and Gorgonzola

1 pound *mezzani* (or substitute ziti, penne, or long
    macaroni)
5 to 7 ounces Gorgonzola cheese
1/3 to 1/2 cup walnuts, quartered
1 tablespoon butter
Salt (for pasta water)
Parsley, if desired, for garnish

Bring 4 quarts of salted water to a full boil and add pasta.
Cook according to package directions.

Meanwhile, cut the Gorgonzola into small pieces and put
into a large pan together with the butter and about three-
fourths of the walnuts. Set the pan aside.

When the pasta is done, remove it from the stove and turn
the burner to high. Drain pasta, reserving about 1 cup of the
cooking water. Immediately add the hot pasta and 1/4 to
1/2 cup of the hot pasta water to the cheese mixture in the
large pan. Place the pan on the hot burner for about 1
minute, stirring to blend. Add a little more hot pasta water, if
necessary, to achieve creaminess.

Sprinkle with chopped parsley and divide among 6 dinner
plates, garnishing with remaining walnuts and parsley sprigs.

Originally published in *The Christian Science Monitor* (February 2, 2005)

15

Artichokes transformed

*Italians know how to make this vegetable's
leaves velvety and tender.*

LADISPOLI, ITALY – Until recently, artichokes as a vegetable had been a great disappointment to me. Excellent as art object or table centerpiece, passable as a paper punch, but as edibles they fell short.

Then I arrived in Italy – a country where the average cook could make tree bark taste agreeable; imagine what they can do with the artichoke. By the time it arrives on your plate here, virtually the entire bulb is melt-on-your-tongue velvety and irresistibly flavorful. An alternative recipe creates a more crunchy leaf, but you can eat the entire leaf without any convulsive jiggering of the mandible.

By the time we set out for *la sagra del carciofo romanesco* (festival of the Roman artichoke) in Ladispoli one Saturday morning last year, my attitude toward this spike-edged vegetable had been transformed.

Ladispoli is a seaside town about a half-hour drive northwest from Rome. By reputation, and owing to the nutrient-rich volcanic soil of the area, the local artichokes are among the best in Italy. Ladispoli's annual artichoke festival, held for three days in April since 1950, is hugely popular, attracting tens of thousands of people each year.

When we arrived, the first thing I did was search for an artichoke grower. I spotted one immediately. Tall and straight-backed, deeply tanned from long workdays in the sun, Arduino Moretti stood serenely at the front of his small booth next to stacked wooden crates overflowing with artichokes.

Originally from the central Italian region of Marche, Mr. Moretti moved to Ladispoli in the 1960s to grow artichokes. Today, he, the four members of his family, and one hired worker produce about 50,000 of the green and purple delicacies each year.

The Mediterranean artichoke season runs from December to April. Artichokes are relatively simple to cultivate, according to Moretti, but cold is their biggest enemy. Only a few degrees drop in temperature and a crop can be ruined. Last year's weather was so mild, they began gathering artichokes around Christmastime, Moretti said.

The vegetable, in fact, is the bud of a flower of a perennial thistle bush. Each plant produces many buds and, when mature, must be picked by hand. (Moretti's large hands are an exhibit themselves: lined, calloused, and stained from handling the artichoke's tough, iron-rich, purplish petals.)

The earliest artichoke buds on the bush are most prized. They are extraordinarily flavorful and tender. The plants

How to Live in Italy

continue to sprout new buds over the remaining season, but their size diminishes with each picking.

Next we wandered toward the food court, where workers under two large tents were cooking deep-fried artichokes on demand for a steady flow of customers drawn by the delicious aroma. In an adjacent booth, men roasted artichokes in a covered grill. This southern Italian method uses a seasoning of olive oil and mint leaves, which causes the artichoke to become succulently tender with a smoked flavor. Artichokes can also be buried in the hot ashes of an open fire and cooked slowly for a couple hours.

We ended the day with a must-see festival program: "Cooking It Well: All the ways to clean, cook, and decorate *il carciofo romanesco.*"

The master of ceremonies introduced himself as a major-domo and member of Ladispoli's cultural association. The variety of artichoke grown in Ladispoli, he said, is the Romanesco, sometimes called Mammolo. It's a hybrid of the Sezze and the Campagnano. He then offered the following tips:

> The artichoke is a flower and should be eaten before it blooms. Choose ones that are still closed and haven't begun to open.

> Only the first two inches of the stem are good for eating, the remainder is too tough. The stems are best for making paté: Cook for at least two hours in water, with a generous amount of olive oil and season with salt and red and black pepper. Then purée.

In frying artichokes, the choice of flour for coating is important. The Japanese have been experimenting with different kinds of flour and have had success with the variety called Manitoba. It's also important that the artichokes and the batter are kept very cold before frying, to enhance the texture.

Our expert also told us that to cook artichokes evenly, we should keep the oil at a temperature no higher than 320 degrees F. For this reason, it's best to use a thermostat-controlled fryer.

I haven't been disappointed with an artichoke since.

Carciofi Alla Romana (Roman Artichokes)

12 artichokes
2 to 3 garlic cloves, minced
1/2 cup nipitella (an Italian herb also known as
    Calamintha nepeta) leaves, chopped, fresh (may
    substitute mint or thyme)
1/4 cup seasoned bread crumbs
1 cup plus 2 tablespoons olive oil, divided
Salt and pepper, to taste

Peel the first two or three layers of tough outer leaves from the artichokes (until the petals are mostly white), and discard. Slice off the top green part. With a small knife, remove the small thorny center beard of the artichoke. Slice off the stems. Keep the first two inches of the stem for cooking, discard the rest. (If not cooking immediately, place the artichokes in a bowl of water with a few slices of lemon.)

Mix together the minced garlic, chopped herbs, bread crumbs, 2 tablespoons olive oil, salt, and pepper.

With a small spoon, gently pry open the heart of the artichoke and insert approximately 1 teaspoon of the filling mixture.

Place the prepared artichokes, upside down, close together in a pot. If cooking the stems, cut into one-inch sections and place in the pot. Add 1 cup olive oil and enough water to reach halfway up the sides of the vegetables. Sprinkle with a little salt and pepper and place on the stove over medium heat. While cooking, periodically add water as necessary to maintain the halfway level, occasionally stirring the oil-water mixture to coat the artichokes. Cook at least an hour, or until tender. Can be served either warm or cold. Serves 6.

Carciofi fritti (Fried Artichokes)

  6 artichokes
  1 cup flour
  2 eggs, beaten
  Oil, enough for deep frying
  Salt and pepper, to taste
  Lemon, to taste

Prepare the artichokes (as above). Slice each artichoke lengthwise into sections (four to eight, depending on size). Lightly dredge the artichoke sections in flour, then in the beaten eggs. Bring the oil to a temperature of 320 degrees F. and drop in the artichokes. Fry until golden brown (a few minutes). Remove and place on paper towels to absorb excess oil. Season with salt, pepper, and lemon. Best served warm. Serves 6.

Originally published in *The Christian Science Monitor* (June 4, 2008)

16

The everlasting Chianina cows

Call me sappy and sentimental, if you will, but I really like cows. As a little girl gazing through the farmyard fence, still blissfully unaware that such attributes are not always the most useful in a Darwinian world, I admired their wide soft eyes and gentle ways.

So I write this bittersweet account of the great white bovine of the central Apennines with a mixture of joy and sadness. I learned their story yesterday when I went to the annual festival in their honor in the village of Bettolle near Siena, Tuscany. Credit for the facts here go primarily to Il Consorzio di Tutela Del Vitellone Bianco Dell'Appennino Centrale (consortium for the protection of white veal of the central Apennines)

The giant white cows, Chianina breed, are the largest in the world. The heavy weight crown, according to Wikipedia, goes to an 8-year-old male, Donetto, in 1955, weighing in at 3,800 pounds plus (almost two tons). The cows originate from the Valdichiana valley in Tuscany and date back to the ancient times of the Etruscans, and to Imperial Rome. Prized not only for their size but for their snowy coats, the bovines were used in triumphal parades and also, not so happily, on temple altars as sacrifices to the gods.

In appearance they are recognizable by the pure white coat, the dark pigmentation of the nose and tongue, their slight, agile heads, short horns, long and cylindrical bodies, wide hips, and legs unusually long for a cow.

Because of their massive heft and strength and docile temperament, Italian farmers and others used them over the centuries for plowing fields and pulling carts and wagons. But after WWII, economic hard times struck Italian farmers hard. Giving up their land in large numbers, many migrated elsewhere to survive. It was then that the fate of the virtually abandoned Chianina hit a moment of peril. Their numbers fell to a dangerously low level. Extinction threatened.

But in the 1990s, the few Valdichiana farmers who still had the great cows began to understand the value of their now rare animals. They joined together to protect and breed the cows. Here, they realized, they had one of humanity's historical treasures.

Not to mention, a very good eat.

The farmers, and butchers had learned to enjoy the meat of the cows – the veal from the calves and the thick steaks known as "bistecca alla fiorentina" from the more mature – are considered among the most delicious by meat lovers worldwide.

Yesterday, in a butcher display stand in Bettolle, the beef steak was listed at more than 23 euro a kilogram ($28 or 19 pounds sterling), and the veal is also pricey. The cows themselves are now bred in many other places in the world, including Asia, Russia, Australia and North and South America.

Yesterday, the final phase of the three-day festival sponsored by the the Friends of the Chianina Association, the featured event was a parade from the town church through the main street. Starring in the procession were two Chianina cows dutifully pulling an old wooden cart. It was decorated colorfully in the style of a wedding. Two actors were perched on top, re-enacting the roles of a bride and groom – a restaging of a rural matrimonial tradition from medieval times.

The cows also were playing an ancient role as they effortlessly, it seemed, towed the heavy cart through the streets. The other, relatively recent role the hardy Chianina now have been cast to play is ongoing – star entree on the menu at your favorite nearby steakhouse.

Originally published on *Demotix.com* (May 30, 2010)

PART THREE

Observing Italians

*What is the fatal charm of Italy? What do we find
there that can be found nowhere else? I believe it is a
certain permission to be human, which other places,
other countries, lost long ago.*

ERICA JONG (*TRAVEL & LEISURE* MAGAZINE)

17

Body beautiful

Angela stands next to me, two bulging, green and pink, thermal picnic bags and an equally overstuffed backpack below her on the sidewalk. Swaying sleepily against her arm is her eight-year-old boy, Rocco, and hovering at a precisely calculated distance yards away in all the ambivalent befuddlement of male puberty is her 14-year-old, Federico. It's 7:45 on a hot July morning and we are waiting for a *Polizia* bus to take us to a beach south of Rome.

The wife of a policeman, Angela has invited me along on this group excursion. During the hot months of July and August, the police buses shuttle officers' families from inland locations to the lidos reserved especially for them at local beaches.

Each summer, in the four years since I moved to Italy, Angela and her husband have told me I was welcome to come along on the police beach bus. But still I'm feeling a bit shy and uneasy as a newcomer. Then the big blue bus arrives and I follow Angela onboard along with two dozen other moms, kids and various relatives. It's such a friendly, cheerful group that I begin to relax.

The bus isn't luxurious but the upholstered highbacked seats are comfortable and all is sparkling clean. Cool air flows from the air conditioner. The driver, an off-duty officer, cranks up the volume on the radio tuned to a Top 40 mix, many of them American or British hits. Beside me, Angela, beautiful and one of the busiest moms I've ever met, is soon half dozing in some rare moments of maternal downtime.

Gazing out the tinted windows as we pass through south-central Italian countryside of gently rolling hills, green fields, olive groves and vineyards, my mind settles into a lazy contemplation. Memories of favorite beaches in Southern California play through my mind. In particular I'm wrestling with that longstanding philosophical dilemma for the female gender – bikini versus one-piece.

It takes a bit of searching on Italian beaches, in my experience, to spot many women wearing one-pieces. Here the bikini is the costume of choice for most. So if you insist on wearing a demure torso coverall in beachwear, as I did last summer, you may feel surprisingly conspicuous. There I was, meekly covered up, and surrounding me were all those other women of every shape, perfect, imperfect and most imperfect, all so... *exposed*.

Don't they know the rule, I sniffed prudishly, the one mandating that women of a certain age or weight must absolutely not appear on public beaches with anything bare other than the tips of their noses? What an amazing liberation from the loony tyranny of the fitness and fashion police! Observing the sisterhood around me that day, I felt rising admiration, a touch of envy, and a wave of disappointment in my own wimpiness.

As our bus arrives in front of a low white building, my reverie fades and curiosity about my day trip surroundings takes its place. The tri-color flag of Italy is flying over the entry portico. Just inside to the right is the ubiquitous espresso bar that also is stocked with juices, sodas and snacks. On the left is a large dining area with a few dozen tables and chairs. Directly ahead is an open terrace flanked by cabanas, bathrooms and showers. Beyond, I see the beach and the blue dazzle of the sea.

Waving me on, Angela lines up to pay the nominal fees for daily rental of lounge chairs and sun umbrellas. Soon we are unpacking our towels and settling in under the shade of the umbrella. All around us others are doing the same. As the shedding of outerwear begins, just as I expected, I see that almost all the women are wearing bikinis.

And today, having summoned my inner Joan of Arc, I'm bravely doing the same.

Folding away my sundress, I ease myself and my bare mid-section down – a bit too quickly – onto my chair. For the next half hour, I chat with Angela as we people-watch. The demographics break out quickly. Clutching their beach toys, children tear off toward the water. Teenagers unerringly gravitate toward one another, and parents, grandparents and the rest of us homestead our chairs and stretch out on beach towels in our chosen subgroups.

Soon Angela is dozing again. I listen to the lapping of the low waves and gaze at the distant horizon, in the usual fashion. After a bit, I begin to feel restless. I consider taking a walk along the surf but mentally squirm as I realize I 'm still feeling conspicuous in my bikini – *all my bodily imperfections are on display for an ogling world to see!*

Sitting cross legged and straight-spined as a yogi in my chair, I isometrically tug in my waistline, trying for flat abs. Good luck with that! I give myself an inner pep talk like a coach pumping up his players at halftime. *Stand up! Stride across that beach! You can do it! Suck it in, suck it up, tuck it under! Oh the heck with it, just get up and go!*

And I do.

As I stroll along the surf, the sunwarmed water splashing deliciously over my toes, I realize the obvious – no one is watching me and even if so, what's the problem? And I feel that unique and particular sense of physical freedom and well-being that comes to us only through a liberated and direct encounter between our bodily selves and nature.

With my self-absorption fading, I begin to observe the people I'm passing. A young father is stretched out stomach to the wet sand next to his toddler daughter and they are digging a little hole with their fingers – perhaps to China? A group of teenagers are languidly tossing around a beach ball where, in their exclusive world within a world, they have eyes only for one another. A grandmother in her golden eighties – she's wearing a one-piece – totters after her diaper-clad grandson who is himself tottering happily along in front of her.

The human body. Here it is, healthy and frail, beautiful and homely, all weight groups, all ages, in full, relaxed display everywhere you look. In the words of the poet W.H. Auden (who himself lived in Italy for ten years) writing about the body – "so simply, publicly there."

September 2005

18

Diving in

Relaxing in the shade of an umbrella on a beach in Sardinia, I turned my head in response to something appearing in my peripheral vision. A teenage girl was striding toward the water's edge. Tall and adolescent thin she waded into the sun-sparkled water without hesitating a moment. Then in one swift and graceful motion, her knees bent, her arms rose, her hands pointed forward, and she soared up and over headfirst into the waves.

One magical moment that felt like the essence of freedom and being. "Oh, I have to do that!" I thought to myself, as if I were answering an imperative command from some sort of life supervisor.

Never much of a swimmer, over the years I had fallen into couch potato habits on trips to the beach. In between tan-seeking intervals stretched out motionless on a beach towel,

I read or dozed or people watched in the shadow of a sun umbrella. Now and then I might stroll to the water's edge and dabble my toes in the gentle lapping of the sea.

That summer day on the island of Sardinia last year changed my ways. More than admiration, I felt a driving surge of envy as I saw the girl's joy as she dived. I felt I must know that feeling myself.

The beaches of the island of Sardinia are famous for their clear water of a particularly beautiful blue color. As amazing, the clear shallows of one to three feet stretch outward from the sand for a hundred or more yards. For those of us who don't swim as easily as the fish, here we can relax with no worries about the "deep end." We can float and play without fear.

I was soon submerging myself in the warm and shallow depths. Next, seeming a natural progression, I began practicing strokes. Of course, I was no threat to Mark Spitz but that summer I began to feel at ease in the water for the first time.

Before I moved to Italy several years ago, going to beach areas for vacation was not on my agenda. In fact, taking any kind of holiday trip was rare. I was one of the many vacation-challenged Americans described in a recent *Christian Science Monitor* article ("Vacation Challenged America" June 21, 2007):

> Many Americans envy Europeans for their generous vacation time, but would they even use it if they had it?

This year's annual vacation survey by Expedia.com, the travel company, shows that about a third of all working adults in the US don't take all the time they've earned – 14 days on average.

Even when they do, are they really on vacation? Nearly a quarter of those who leave don't totally leave – they're still checking work e-mail or voice mail from under the beach umbrella (the exact figure is 23 percent, up markedly from 16 percent just two years ago).

I'm pleased to report that I've overcome that odd habit. It wasn't all that agonizing, really. When you see a whole country heading out on annual vacations as spontaneously as birds migrating south in winter, following the crowd comes easily.

This year we went on another beach vacation, to Apulia. In recent years, travel writers have been describing this southern Italy region as the new Tuscany. And some our friends here also sang its praises, comparing some of the Apulia beaches and warm waters to those of superstar Sardinia.

As promised, we found some of those beaches. As many do, we carried sun umbrella and beach chairs along and homesteaded a spot on a favorite beach more or less daily for the two-week span of our visit. Is Apulia the new Tuscany or Sardinia's twin? The vacationers we saw there seemed happy enough that it was simply Apulia, with its own particular identity.

What brought Sardinia to mind for me was the fun of diving into the waves headfirst, again. It's become a new habit. I recommend it. Also vacations.

July 2007

19

Neighbors

As I get to know my new neighbors, sometimes they make jokes.

I heard the first one soon after we moved to a different town and into an apartment we bought last summer in a structure built in the 1600s. As historical places go, the town of about 10,000 is significant, but it's not a tourist hot spot. And, as most of the residents were born here, newcomers are fairly conspicuous.

Walking the dogs one morning soon after we arrived, I met an elderly man making his way slowly along the cobblestone sidewalk. Stopping a few feet from me and seemingly fearful, he stared at the two small terriers and the large border collie I was walking and asked, "Have they eaten yet?"

Momentarily I was literally tongue-tied. He was speaking Italian, of course, and I still flounder with the language when I feel confused by something. And I'm also somewhat anxious when I meet people who have a fear of dogs.

"Mi scusi?" I said in confusion, after the long pause.

"Hanno già mangiato?" he repeated. (Have they already eaten?)

This time I understood but still I didn't get the joke. Then he smiled, the mock expression of fear on his face disappearing. Comprehension dawned. I laughed, relieved.

In the months since then I've heard that same joke often when I've met this man on one of the daily dog runs. He's usually on his way to spend a few hours with some other elderly men in the park-like piazza next to where we live. I always laugh politely in response. The line's stale but the kindness wrapped in humor is welcome.

This morning, another joke.

My next door neighbor was passing by under our second floor balcony, taking her own dog out. I've been busily buying plants this springs to hang from the boxes on the railing and to fill floor pots. I called good morning to her and then pointed to a strawberry plant I potted recently. One plump, almost ripe strawberry glistening red, dangled from a long stem.

"Look!" I said proudly.

She smiled and nodded. "You can make a *macedonia*," she called back, laughing and referring to the fresh fruit salad so popular with Italians in summertime.

Her name is Maria and she and her husband and eight-year-old son live in the building adjacent to ours. I see them often on the balcony, the boy playing with their dog, Maria and her husband relaxing or talking to neighbors.

There are only two plants in small boxes at either end of their balcony, both small succulents. That's all. Maria told me one day that her father had a florist shop and she grew up helping him in the shop. Sometimes I ask her for green thumb advice. She always obliges but told me once that her work at her father's shop tired her of plant caretaking. So, though she answers with an expert's ease, her attitude of been-there-and-done-much-too-much-of-that is evident.

And then there are the old women, five or so of them. I'm not being ageist, just factual. They are old, all in their late seventies or eighties, or more. I call them *le signore* and they are my favorite neighbors.

Every day, weather permitting, they come out of their various front doors and walk slowly, very slowly, along the street we all share, placing their feet carefully along the unevenness of the cobblestones. Sometimes they pause to catch their breath or to rest a bad knee or leg as they climb the slight slope of the street at one end. Sometimes they walk with a hand resting on their backs or hips, soothing an ache.

When the weather is fair and the sun warms the day, they sit on the front steps of one of the block's buildings in the morning and late afternoon. It's the feminine gender counterpart to the men gathering in the piazza. Both are old neighborhood social traditions handed down for generations.

The old women were the first to welcome us when we arrived. In the months of renovation of our new apartment before we moved in, we would often see them when we stopped by on inspection trips. They watched our comings and goings curiously, a little warily. Franco invariably stopped and greeted them. Speaking in dialect, they responded politely, though minimally at first, but each time became increasingly friendly.

I see them now daily usually but I still don't know all of their names. When they nod at me and say, *Buon giorno, signora*, it's enough for now that I reply in kind.

The joke that *le signore* share with me is subtle, unspoken and, perhaps imaginary on my part. It's something in their eyes that seems to smile out at me when I stop to chat with them, something that wonders a little – but only a little – at this outsider. It's okay that you're different, this witty something in their eyes tells me, it's okay that I don't understand a word you just said. It's okay.

The old woman I see most often lives in the apartment above ours. She stays with her son, Lorenzo, who is married to a young woman from Eastern Europe. A skilled jack of all trades in home maintenance, Lorenzo is often in demand. I learned his name quickly. The sound of it ringing out – Lorenzo! Lorenzo! – by someone outside looking for him is almost as regular as the church bells pealing several times a day at the nearby convent and church opposite each other on the square.

Lorenzo also owns a tiny shop only a few doors away. The entry is plain, unmarked, with a rose bush climbing up the stone wall. He stocks some household items and sells *bombole*, the butane gas cannisters used for small heaters and stoves. We rented one from him ourselves for a couple of

How to Live in Italy

weeks after we moved in while waiting for the plumber to finish connecting our new central heating system.

Most days except Sunday, Lorenzo's mother sits in the shop, or on the front steps if the sun is shining, minding the store. A few of the other old women stop in for a while too. They sit and talk with each other, or sometimes just sit without talking, together greeting anyone who comes in.

Recently I learned that one of the sweetest of the old women is moving away. She can neither see nor hear well but once she determine who or what goes there, she is warmly polite and solicitous. Her family is a marvel of four generations living together, from great grandmother to great granddaughter. They now are too many for the apartment they share, she told me. They've bought a larger place at the other end of town. I told her I was sorry she was leaving and she said she was too.

"I've lived here sixty years," she said. "It isn't fair." But she was smiling, as if this late-arriving change is only another joke, this one made by the funniest comedian of all, life itself.

May 2006

20

Just standing around buying things

One of hundreds of shoppers, a young man wearing a baseball cap squats on his heels measuring the length of a desk. He's talking on his cell phone and describing his find to someone on the other end. A young couple walk by so engrossed in each other and their conversation, they don't see anything or anyone. A thirtyish mom with her dark red hair cut short is browsing the shelves in a corner of the housewares department. She seems oblivious to the toddler on her hip who is screaming loud enough to wake Socrates. No one else takes much notice of the wailing either – it's a temper tantrum-friendly kind of place.

I'm standing in an office furniture department, scrutinizing a small computer stand on rollers that seems to me just the right size to place next to my desk at home, I loosen the belt on my coat and unbutton it. It's cozily warm. Unlike some stores in Italy in wintertime where the clerks sometimes stand hugging themselves and shivering in unheated shops of budget-conscious management – energy costs are so high – it's never cold in this one.

It's Thursday evening and I'm in the IKEA store on the Anagnina highway on the outskirts of Rome. IKEA has two stores in the metropolitan area, one north of the city, one south. I've only ever been to this one in the south and it's usually jampacked with shoppers. Italians, surrounded by more priceless antiquities per square foot by far than any other populace in the world, seem to like these huge boxy-homely stores that could be an antonym for what most people imagine when they think of Italy. The company already has twelve retail sites in the country and a couple of new ones on the way.

On the other hand, I muse to myself, perhaps the famously design conscious Italians appreciate the priority of functional design that is at the heart of IKEA's success. Much of the merchandise is dismountable and easy to fit into the trunk or back of the car, and then reliably easy to construct once you get it home.

I decide to call my sister-in-law Silvia, an architecture graduate and artist, and ask if she approves of IKEA products.

"Yes," she says. "The design is modern but it's also a little bit artisanal and the pricing is democratic." Then she laughs and adds, "I think, perhaps more than anything, it's the price."

Whatever, along with McDonald's, which has restaurants scattered across Rome and a few hundred more across the rest of the country, it seems this icon of globalization is here and growing. As conspicuous here as Hollywood movies predominant in theaters, and the new shopping malls popping up across the landscape as if spread by a flu bug.

I suppose I sound grumpy as I say that. The whine of someone who wants to turn the clock back, wants Italy to be only a tourist fantasy of Roman ruins, delicious food and wine, and oh-so-charming countryside dotted with pretty little villages. Well, yeah, sometimes I do, I admit. But the Italians have to share some of the blame for this. They themselves refuse to succumb meekly to becoming the usual identical, conforming consumer drones.

The truth is it's the Italian people themselves who've created my discontent with the encroachment of modern marketing here. It's the way they live their daily lives, the way they insist on valuing "ordinary good living" as the norm, it's this that truly makes Italy a place where visitors from all over the world want to come and then want to return again and again. So how can I or anyone else be blamed if we get a little worried when the usual suspects of popular mass culture begin to turn up here also?

Still, being the singular people they are – certainly I'm not the first one to describe them so – Italians have a way of transforming even these ever-replicating fast food and furniture chains into something uniquely theirs.

Visit one of those new shopping malls here and you will see the same classic Italian social style as you see everywhere else in the country. At lunchtime, the stores empty as the Italians stop shopping and fill up the restaurants, pizzerias and the *tavola calda*. It's a leisurely time that stretches into a chatty lingering over espresso, and standing around in the mall's open spaces visiting with each other just as if they were in the piazzas of their own neighborhoods and villages. You might suppose the managers of the shops would be annoyed by this. But, often, they too are Italian, so probably not.

There are some business types who look at this behavior and call it chaos. I just look at it and know I like it.

———————————————

Originally published on *foreignremarks.com* (December 2006)

How to Live in Italy

21

Olive trees, olives and, oh yes, the oil

"Beppe!" I call to the man several yards in front of us, "Do you have a favorite tree?" We are making our way across ground cover of grass and wild flowers that sprawls through his olive grove high on the side of an Apennine mountain. Beppe turns and points behind us toward a thriving, broadly branched tree that stood fifteen to twenty feet high.

"Why?" I ask. And wait, feeling as eager to hear his response as someone who seeks out a wise man and begs him to reveal the true meaning of life. Surely his words will be as rich as the poetic aura of the age old panorama surrounding us, with snow peaked mountain ranges filling the horizon, and a cloudless blue sky above.

"*È il migliore produttore*," Beppe shouts back. "*Mi fa duecento chili di olive all'anno.*" (Translation – It's the best producer. It gives me more than 450 pounds of olives a year.)

Bye bye fantasy. The answer is classic, down-to-earth Beppe (short for Giuseppe). A retired nurse, he has a quick dry wit that has been peppering our interview for the past three hours. "He knows his olive trees better than he knows his children," a mutual friend told us when I had asked for a recommendation of someone to interview about growing olives.

When we called Beppe a couple of weeks later, he immediately invited us to lunch. So on this Sunday in late April we had driven to his home in Vico nel Lazio. The medieval village is more than 2000 feet above sea level on the slopes of Mt. Ernici. It's home to about 2000 inhabitants and is located just above thickly forested slopes approximately forty miles east of Rome. The higher elevation deepens the sense of being in a place a world apart.

Vico, with its tightly compact labyrinth of streets and historical structures, is closely encircled by ancient walls. They feature three massive portals and, amazingly, twenty-five battlement towers. Beppe was born here as were generations of his family before him. It's unlikely there's anyone in this village he doesn't know.

I'm feeling especially pleased with myself to have found my way to him as part of my quest to find out as much as I can about olive trees, olives and olive oil. To learn the history of these ancient trees and how to grow and to take care of them has become something of a passion. I've fallen under their spell, just as millions of others have who've visited Italy, or other Mediterranean or middle eastern countries where the olive groves are ubiquitous. I have a long list of questions for Beppe.

How to Live in Italy

For lunch, Beppe and his wife Lucia serve us angel hair pasta with fresh asparagus and prosciutto, all handmade or home supply. The red wine we drink comes from the vineyard of their son. On the table are two bottles of olive oil, fresh from Beppe's grove. One bottle holds oil *più amaro* (more bitter), this for Beppe's taste. The other bottle is filled with oil *più dolce* (sweeter), to suit the preference of Lucia.

Later, Beppe shows us the storeroom nearby where he keeps his annual yield of oil of approximately 1000 liters. The gold-green liquid is stored in large metal canisters. About 100 liters is kept aside, he says, for the family's use through the coming year. The remainder of the artisan supply is sold locally to friends and neighbors, as is the custom with many private grove owners.

The Grand Tour

In the afternoon, following a short tour of the village center, Beppe drives with us about a quarter mile back down the mountain road leading into Vico. Off a small side lane is the seven-acre grove (400 olive trees) of which he is so proud. Beppe has these trees thanks to his grandfather who gave the grove to him, his first grandson.

His grandfather bought it in 1933 with money he himself made by working in Cincinnati, Ohio for several years. He was part of a mass migration out of Italy at the time of thousands of Italians who were literally starving in their impoverished home territories. Beppe's grandfather worked in the limestone quarries in the Cincinnati area where manual laborers were much in demand.

Now standing with us under his beloved trees, Beppe is happy to give us a tutorial.

"The tree talks," Beppe begins. "It says, 'Look at my strength and leave the burden to me.' There are trees that are majestic, generous. There are some that really are more than a thousand years old," he adds, stressing the word really.

The grove where we stand is just at the extreme edge of possible elevation in this area to grow olive trees, Beppe continues. Any higher and the freezing temperatures would damage the trees. Because of this, he says he chooses varieties of trees that are resistant to cold, specifically *Leccino* and *Trana*.

When pruning, Beppe says he has to understand if the tree has the strength to feed all its branches or not. If not, then some must be pruned. Each tree varies in its fruitbearing from year to year, he explains, so it's important to remember with every tree how one year one part has fruit, one part no. This way when he prunes them annually, Beppe says, he remembers not to cut the part that didn't bear olives the year before.

Also, the wind affects each tree's growth. A branch may not produce anything because of too much wind, so the next year Beppe says he has to remember not to prune it because it is still strong from the long rest. There are two kinds of branches, he explains, categorizing them as male and female. The distinction is in the leaves. The male branch leaves have the smooth side toward the north, the female branch leaves' smooth surface is to the south.

When he cuts off the small, new branches, Beppe says he must prune away all the males. It's important to remember always to leave at least one new female per permanent branch because only the female ones bear fruit.

All of this, Beppe says, he learned from his grandfather.

The grove also has cherry, prune, and apple trees. Wild chicory with its small, blue flowers pokes through here and there in the rough grass. The adjoining field is rocky but Beppe's ground has been cleared. The stones are all piled in a long row on one side, giving the appearance of a low wall. The sum effect is a visual poem of man in harmonious relationship with nature. It's easy to see why Beppe calls the grove his *paradiso*.

As we reluctantly leave the grove and walk to the car, Beppe continues to tell us stories about his grandfather and the times they spent together. His grandfather had left school after only the third grade, but Beppe describes the teaching he got from him as his "university." And the lessons weren't just about trees, he says, but about life.

"My grandfather told me, 'With olive oil the bad goes down and the good rises. This is also how it is with human beings. It seems the bad people go up, but that's not true – they will always go down.'"

I ask Beppe if his grandfather liked America. "Yes," he answers.

Why? I ask, once again – naively – eager for some profound words.

"At least there they were eating," Beppe quips.

Originally published on *foreignremarks.com* (February 2007)

22

Dream house

Of the hundreds of images I saw on a recent visit to the ancient *Villa Romana del Casale* in Sicily, I recall most vividly the real life, forlorn figure of Valerio Salerno. Under southern Italy's hot Mediterranean sun that is doing its usual work of creating sweltering temperatures, Salerno has taken refuge in the shade of small tree near the famed ruins' entrance.

I have already turned down his offer to serve as our guide but he is refusing to go away.

"Don't listen to her, come with me! I'm better than any book," he calls to Franco. He has spotted the red-covered, guidebook in my hands. We've just bought it at one of the many vendor stalls lining the pedestrian lane leading to the villa.

Salerno appears to be middle-aged and is wearing a well-worn and blue blazer over gray-brown sweater and trousers. Atop his head, a white Alpine hat with a wilted black feather in the band adds a distinguishing touch. The overall impression is of someone who could use the money.

But it's not just the twenty euro he is asking for his services that prompted my no. It's my worry that he will distract me from really seeing what we've traveled here to see – almost 38,000 square feet of mosaics in near optimal condition. The artwork covers more than forty rooms of this 1700 year-old Roman villa.

Excavated only a few decades ago, the villa is considered by scholars to be one of the world's great treasures. In 1997, UNESCO officially endorsed this view and designated the villa as a World Heritage Site.

Standing at the entrance of what remains of what was once someone's palatial-size dreamhouse, I now feel a bit overwhelmed. The villa is in a rural area just outside the small town of Piazza Armerina. It's an isolated spot, unpretentious with none of the fussiness to be expected considering the villa's renown status.

The historical importance and unique value of the site seem disconcertingly underserved, somewhat like discovering an emerald in the pocket of a comfortable old bathrobe. The ruins' structure itself, now covered by modern, protective roofing, sprawls confusingly in various directions. The floor plan isn't immediately apparent to my inexpert eye.

At the official kiosk near the parking lot we had tried to rent an audio guide but were told all the English versions were out, and my Italian isn't up to the native language version. Hearing Salerno's persistent sales pitch, I re-think my situation and surrender.

In a string of efficiently truncated English phrases surprisingly well-enunciated, Salerno first runs through his curriculum vitae. "My mom, she born here," he says, waving vaguely toward a nearby hilltop. "She saw most of the work. I've been interviewed two times," he adds with evident pride, mentioning the name of a major US newspaper.

The villa ruins are overlaid with a kind of do-it-yourself type of touring system. It consists of dozens of wood plank walkways elevated a few inches above the floor mosaics, guiding visitors from one room to the next. Providing a different perspective here and there, are also short flights of metal stairs leading to raised viewing walkways. A thin layer of dust covers the mosaics, but the bright colors and precise delineation of the complex designs are striking.

As soon becomes apparent, Salerno is a jealous guardian of the villa. "You cannot walk there!" hc calls sternly to one visitor who has just stepped off the wooden walkway onto the mosaic-covered floor.

The artists who created the yards and yards of priceless artworks under our feet were master mosaicists from North Africa, according to the Princeton Encyclopedia of Classical Sites (edited by Richard Stillwell). Stillwell describes the artists' style as expressive of *a mood at times rash and bloody and at times veiled with sadness.*

The range of the subject matter is wide. There are hunting scenes from Africa, and a variety of birds and animals – dogs, horses, lions, panthers, elephants, goats, antelope, wild boar, hares, ostriches, hippopotamuses and rhinoceroses. In some scenes, animals are shown on gangplanks of ships, on the way to serve as entertainment for crowds in ancient Rome's Coliseum. In others, there are chariot races, horse races, and sea scenes with small boats and winged figures fishing with nets.

Some of the most impressive mosaics illustrate mythological tales. Among these are the twelve labors of Hercules, Ulysses confronting the one-eyed colossus Polyphemus, Orpheus playing his lyre, and scenes of tributes being made to the goddess of the hunt, Diana. In contrast are the scenes of ordinary families and home life, husbands and wives, children and slaves.

Then there are the exotic scenes – women dancing, and the often-mentioned and surprising mosaic on the gymnasium floor featuring ten girls in bikinis.

Leading us past this amazing variety of scenes, Salerno's voice falls into a monotone, reciting a list that at times is unintentionally comic: "Ash, bench, fountain, oven," he says, pointing with a blue ballpoint pen that he uses as a lecturer might. "Tiger, elephant, horse. Man on horse chasing animals, wounded man on ground rescued by friends." And waving toward a figure whose hand is touching his forehead, "Man with headache."

Much has been written also about the architectural design of the villa itself. It has four separate sections, each one higher than the preceding one. These include reception areas, a gymnasium and a series of rooms with hot and cold thermal baths, two huge atriums, a dining room of almost 2700 square feet, guest rooms, and private, family quarters with separate apartments. It appears no expense was spared in the villa's construction, and when it was completed, according to UNESCO, it was so grand and lavish it set a new and unparalleled level of luxury for Roman villas.

The Villa Romana del Casale – *Casale* means farm or farmhouse and also refers to the local name for the area – is located just about midcenter of the island of Sicily. Here the topography is a broad plain which has been devoted to cultivation of wheat and barley since ancient times.

The exact identity of the villa's owner-builder is lost to history, scholars say, though perhaps some clue may be buried away under the tons of dirt over area that is still to be excavated. Some speculate that the owner may have been either one of the Roman emperors, or a high ranking military officer. Several other owners followed in succeeding centuries, and the villa suffered major damage during the many wars fought on the island.

Then, in the 12th century, the final blow was delivered via a landslide that buried the entire structure. Only a few segments were left jutting above ground. Farmers planted crops atop the new dirt deposit and over time everyone pretty much forgot the villa existed. The process of re-discovery came first in the late 1800s when scavengers began digging up pieces of mosaics and columns to sell or use. In the1920s Italian archaeologists began the major excavation.

At the end of the tour, Salerno stands quietly, his jacket now removed and folded neatly over one arm. He politely answers my last few questions. Pointing to my notebook, he says, "We need a school. We need a school for training, an archaeologist school. Put that there."

July 2004

23

Rome's Vittoriano
and its critics

Not long ago I was passing in front of The Vittoriano, the gigantic, white monument in Piazza Venezia in Rome that guidebooks often refer to as "the typewriter," and I recalled a wacky scene about it from an Italian movie I saw a few years ago.

The 2002 movie, *L'ora di religione* (The Religion Hour), directed by Marco Bellocchio, follows the spiritual agonizing of a successful and atheistic Italian painter after he learns that the Vatican is considering canonizing his murdered mother. The acclaimed film is especially fascinating for the insider look it offers of cosmopolitan Italian life. One of these glimpses is a gem of conversation in which the painter is approached by a stranger who recognizes him while they are sitting in a hospital waiting room.

The very sad, unknown man is an architect. He begins the conversation by talking about beauty and how it is said that it drives us mad. On the contrary, he said, for him it is ugliness that has driven him mad.

"Every time I went past The Vittoriano, it angered me so much that I could barely control myself. Many think that I am a nihilist, an anarchist, but they don't understand. They don't understand that it is the ugliness of the monument that disgusts me, not its patriotic meaning. No I can't bear it, I have found that its ugliness is blocking the imagination of architects throughout the world, it frightens and terrorizes them."

The man then adds:

"So I decided to blow it up... the monument, so it would no longer exist. But it was too much for me. And it is because of this that I am sick."

As I discovered when I went searching online recently, the view of the mad architect in this darkly comic scene is commonly shared by architects in real life. In his much quoted 1998 essay "Outrage," bemoaning the monument's design, noted architect and critic Peter Davey opens with, "In the ancient heart of the mother of cities, there is an ugly excrescence that totally ignores all the lessons of urbanity and townscape that Rome has to teach."

A subsequent sentence is excerpted with top rank regularity in search engine results online: "The monument was chopped with terrible brutality into the immensely complicated fabric of the hill."

Davey's closing words, however, acknowledge the most important and determinant fact about The Vittoriano. It is also known as "The Altar of the Nation." It is here to stay because it honors the nation's military and houses the actual remains of Italy's unknown soldier. As such it is the most sacred secular shrine in the country. And it is this most poignant reality that relegates all the criticism – learned though it is – to the sidelines as just so much chatter.

How the monument came to be is a complex and lengthy story. The guidebooks will tell you the basics. An Italian architect, Giuseppe Sacconi, won an international competition to design the Victor Emmanuel II monument in 1884. It took more than two decades to build and was inaugurated in 1911 on the fiftieth anniversary of the unification of Italy.

In another article I found online (20 plus pages that were worth every centesimo of the 23 euro I paid to download them), university geography professors David Atkinson and Denis Cosgrove meticulously trace the history of the monument over a 75-year period, beginning with its inception.

To cut to the chase – if I may be so crass about this exquisite scholarly work – Atkinson and Cosgrove narrate the birth, design, building and early decades of The Vittoriano as a complex interplay of powerful conflicting forces. It originated with the noble idea to build a great monument to the unification of Italy and to the king who reigned over that long and bloody process. It was boycotted every step of the way by the strongly opposed-to-it-all Vatican – the sulky loser in that unification process. And finally and dramatically, the monument and all it was originally intended to honor was co-opted and exploited heavily by Mussolini and his Fascist followers during the time between the two World Wars.

But perhaps the simplest explanation of how the monument came to be the grand offense it is to architects worldwide – as Bellocchio's own fictional crazed architect asserted – came to me from an architect-artist friend of mine. I had sent her a text message asking for some information about Sacconi, the obscure designer of the monument.

"But why do you want to talk about this disgusting thing?" she wrote back. "It is urban architecture used as a representation of power."

Learning all this has had a surprising effect on me, the typical ill-informed, passing tourist. It's made me feel something akin to sympathy for this much derided monument, if it's possible to feel such for an inanimate and gargantuan mass of white marble. Like an ant contemplating an elephant – and would anyone give that great creature high marks for pleasing design? – ugly or not, I feel amazed and hushed. I'm a bit in awe of all The Vittoriano has been asked to symbolize by its motley committee of creators, and by the burden of ridicule that continues to rain down on it to this day.

Originally published in *Demotix.com* (August 1, 2010)

24

The art of seeing in Cortina

It's a faraway, beautiful place, Cortina, Italy, but it's really very far away for most. So why go?

The famous reason is the skiing. The small town in the Dolomites not only reportedly offers the best slopes in Italy, it ranks among top ski resorts worldwide. So ideal and spectacular is Cortina's mountainous terrain for skiing, it was chosen to host the 1956 winter Olympic Games. On a hill just south of the village, a 177-foot tall ski jump built for those games is still in use.

Almost 100 miles of ski trails weave through Cortina and its surrounds. Of those miles, forty-three wind cross-country through Alpine forests and valley landscapes.

There's another reason tourists head for Cortina, though. It's an open secret among Italians and, judging by the tourists we encountered, still undiscovered by non-

Europeans for the most part. In the late spring when the snow melts away, appearing alongside those ski trails are miles and miles of paths for walking. It's a walking raised to its highest incarnation, one that bears about as much resemblance to the average walk as opening a can of tuna does to deep-sea fishing for Marlin.

We arrived there on a warm mid-August afternoon this year to stay a week with some friends who have a vacation place there. The following morning – very early – we prepared our backpacks and set off for the first big walk. Franco and our friends, a married couple, are passionate and veteran mountain walkers. While studying the area's hiking map the previous evening, they assured me that, in my honor as a novice, our first walk would be an easy one.

Cortina is on the border of two adjoining natural parks that spread across 143 square miles. At various altitudes among the parks' ranges and peaks, some higher than 10,000 feet, are 56 *rifugi*. These are rustic mountain inns whose restaurants and broad terraces are jammed at lunchtime with skiers in winter and hikers and climbers from late June to September.

For the first stage of our walk, we leave our car at a tourism center just outside Cortina and take a kind of taxi. This comfortable mini-van shuttle is one of dozens that run back and forth daily on the restricted-entry, narrow roads of the park, ferrying tourists close to the lower-lying mountain inns. We're headed to the *Ra Stua* inn, elevation 5,472 feet.

Ra Stua is set overlooking a wide, grassy plateau. A mountain stream flows along one side, and slim trunked fir trees bunch around the upper perimeter. The sun is shining, the sky is clear blue, a dozen or so fat brown and white cows graze on what seems more like a well-kept lawn than a field. It's the first of many times during that week, I look around and feel that I am, as one British travel writer put it, "lost in an advert for Swiss chocolate." Every direction I turn the landscape seems impossibly and perfectly paradisaical.

Not stopping at the inn, we begin with a stroll along a wide lane for a quarter of a mile. This turns off on to a narrow path that winds up a steep hillside for about 1,700 feet. Although moving at turtle pace, I am panting when we reach the top. I much favor the gentle incline of the pretty lane we have left behind. As I learn later, we could have followed that easier way all the way to the *rifugio Biella*, (elevation 7,634 feet), where we are headed for lunch. But my companions (slightly maddened by their walking passion I'm beginning to suspect) had chosen the more challenging route.

After a five minute rest we move on. The path becomes more rocky and at times only two-feet wide, but, thankfully, there's no replay of the introductory steep ascent. An hour later, we reach the top of another hill and look down into a wide valley with a small lake shining at the bottom.

On an opposite hillside, a flock of several hundred sheep, attended by three black herding dogs and three shepherds, are moving slowly down toward the water. Single blocks of salt are here and there on the slope and the sheep run to crowd around them. They jostle each other roughly, trying to get their tongues on the saline treat. In this confusion, some lambs are separated from their mothers. It's fascinating to watch the mother sheep bleat loudly until each lost offspring locates its own maternal sound and goes running to be reunited.

Just before 2 pm, we reach the Biella mountain inn. The restaurant inside is packed with hikers lunching on hot pasta dishes, polenta, thick soups and steaks. Conversation is noisy and the big room is warm. We choose, instead, the wide, planked-floor terrace with its scenic views and picnic style tables.

From the inn menu, we order only wine, and later coffee, as is a popular custom. We unpack the prosciutto, salami, cheese, fresh bread, and fresh tomato and basil salad we had brought with us and dig in with the ravenous hunger that comes from walking in the mountains. I pause only long enough to remove my new hiking shoes – their stiff support was wearing painfully on my feet after only an hour into the walk. I'd felt as pleased as a six-year-old when we'd bought them a few days before but now I feel tempted to donate the tortuous things to anyone passing by.

The Biella inn is at the base of the *Croda Del Becco* mountain. It's one of 23 ranges that encircle (crown) Cortina, thus giving rise to its nickname, "Queen of the Dolomites." *Croda Del Becco* was re-christened only recently, I learn, in honor of a herd of Ibex who appeared on the mountain about 20 years ago. Previously, the wild goats had disappeared and were considered extinct in the local area.

Before being renamed, the roundshaped mountain was called, comically, *El Cu de ra Badessa.* Sounds musical enough but in translation, it means "the ass of the Abbess" and was called so "in honor" of a powerful and controversial Mother Superior who lived in the area in the 1400s.

With the *Croda* peak rising almost straight up another 1,600 feet beyond us, I am happy to learn we're not going there. Instead, after our leisurely lunch break, we begin our descent but in a new direction. We walk first for a quarter of a mile along the broad "*Alta Via delle Dolomiti*," a wellknown footpath that extends for almost a hundred miles through the eastern Dolomites.

My elation that all movement now will be downhill, is temporarily squashed when we face another steep ascent before connecting again with the descending trail. I'm told it's a shortcut, as if that's any comfort. But halfway up this ascent, we are rewarded. We hear a Marmot, a European mammal somewhat similar to a groundhog. It is whistling a warning to its nest mates. Without binoculars, all we can see in the distance is a shifting large brown dot near the dirt surface of the Marmots' underground nest. But even so, it's a rare treat – these people-shy, endangered animals are so expert at hiding themselves they are seldom seen by tourists.

Reaching the halfway point of our descent, we stop briefly at another inn, the *Utia de Senes*. Here more animals grazing, this time three plump, squeaky-clean white pigs in company with one cow, the big bronze bell hanging from its neck clanging with every move. All were ranging freely, no fences or barriers anywhere in sight.

From here, we still have several thousand feet to go to get to the bottom. The wide trail is now falling at a fifteen degree angle, the surface covered with loosely packed, fragments of white dolomitic stone. This is hard going for me. We're still above the tree line so the panorama is still stunning but I don't care. My toes, sore to a numblike aching, are colliding with the rigid new leather of my shoes. And I have an over-sized blister rising on my left heel. I slow my pace to a painful limp and comfort myself by vowing I will never scale an altitude higher than our front stairway ever again.

Just before 5 p.m., we are back again full circle to *Ra Stua*, the inn where we'd started. We take our place among a couple of dozen others, mostly families with small children, waiting for the steadily arriving mini vans taxis. I plop down exhausted on the grass and take off my Marquis di Sade footcoverings. Looking around, I see I'm the only one in such piteous shape. Apparently I'm the only greenhorn there, or maybe the only one dumb enough to wear new shoes on a first day's hike. (And I can't resist mentioning, by the way, that the easy walk I'd been promised by my three companions had lasted more than eight hours.)

As it turns out the vow I made to myself as I was limping down the mountainside is short lived. The following day, instead of another walk, I do choose the comfortable option of one of the many ski lifts also in operation during the summer months. They offer the less able, more lazy – or blister afflicted, as in my case – an easy access to the mountain inns. But the following day, rested and with a miracle-of-modern-medicine type bandaid covering the evil blister, I happily throw on my backpack and set off on another segment of the 186 miles of *sentieri* (hiking trails) in the area. And each day after that.

At the end of the week, I'm truly sorry to see this new walking adventure come to an end. I understand why so

many return as if in annual migration to Cortina each
summer.

March 2006

25

St. Michael in the rain

"Do you believe in angels?"

"Why not?" Franco replied, in the enigmatic way he has sometimes when talking about his beliefs.

"What are they," I asked. "What do the Roman Catholics say they are?"

"Spirits of God. Emanations. Messengers," he said following a thread of thought.

"What are the messages?"

"Information, or sometimes just strength for a situation." He paused, recollecting. "Immanuel is somehow God's presence itself."

"I thought St. Michael was the greatest angel?"

"Immanuel isn't an angel…"

And so the conversation continued as we sat at a table yesterday under the narrow awning of a Rome sidewalk cafe.

We had stopped there to take shelter from a surprise rainstorm. Except for two British women who were paying their check at the table next to us, no one else was there. The owner was standing nearby, frowning up at the dark sky. Franco commented to him about the storm.

"It drove everyone away," the man said resentfully, waving toward the empty streets. "They've all gone back to their hotels now."

Shortly before, the streets had been crowded with tourists and shoppers. The skies had been clear, the sun bright. On one of the first warm days of spring, many bars and restaurants had their sidewalk tables set out and awnings unrolled. But the rain and a chilling breeze were disappointing merchants' hopes.

Yesterday was a national holiday in Italy, the celebration of the liberation at the end of World War II. We decided to go into Rome for the afternoon and to stop by an exhibition at Castel Sant'Angelo. The massive, circular castle, also known as Hadrian's Tomb, is within view of St. Peter's Square.

Anyone who has ever seen or toured the castle will now understand the genesis of my angel conversation with Franco. Towering over Castel Sant'Angelo's broad rooftop terrace is a gigantic bronze sculpture of the archangel Michael. In a courtyard inside the castle, another sculpture of the avenging angel, eleven feet high, stands on a pedestal.

The exhibition we had just seen also featured a striking 1600s painting of St. Michael the Archangel by Guido Reni. And so my mind had drifted into a contemplation on the subject of angels.

For me, this kind of mind flow is one of most enjoyable aspects of spending time in Rome. The city is a deluge of imagery. Antiquity surrounds you, its presence every way you turn. And the inextricable mix of modern day living alongside icons and architecture of pagan mythology and early and medieval Roman Catholic religious life spin the mind and whirl it loose from its usual familiar habitat. Thinking can be set free.

Yesterday, mine escaped its reality-bound world awhile to think about angels. Angels as possibilities.

Why not.

Originally published on *foreignremarks.com* (April 2007)

Made in the USA
Lexington, KY
02 August 2013